D1179302

THE WHISKY
COMPANION

Tom Quinn

A THINK BOOK

*Life without whisky is like a
broken pencil – pointless.*

Anon

THINK
BOOKS

A Think Book

First published in Great Britain in 2005 by
Think Publishing
The Pall Mall Deposit
124-128 Barlby Road, London W10 6BL
www.thinkpublishing.co.uk

Distributed in the UK and Ireland by Macmillan Distribution Ltd.
Brunel Road, Houndmills, Basingstoke RG21 6XS

Distributed in the United States and Canada by
Sterling Publishing Co., Inc.
387 Park Avenue South
New York, NY 10016-8810

Text © Think Publishing 2006
Design and layout © Think Publishing 2006
The moral rights of the author have been asserted

Edited by Tom Quinn
Companion team: Tilly Boulter, James Collins, Rica Dearman,
Rhiannon Guy, Emma Jones, Claire Maxted, Lou Millward,
Matt Packer, Sonja Patel, Jo Swinnerton and Malcolm Tait

ISBN-10: 1-84525-011-7
ISBN-13: 978-1-84525-011-9

Printed in Italy by Grafica Veneta S.p.A.
The publishers and authors have made every effort to ensure the accuracy and
currency of the information in *The Whisky Companion*. Similarly, every effort
has been made to contact copyright holders. We apologise for any
unintentional errors or omissions. The publisher and authors disclaim any
liability, loss, injury or damage incurred as a consequence, directly or
indirectly, of the use and application of the contents of this book.

Too much of anything is bad, but too much of good whiskey is barely enough.

Mark Twain

As you leaf your way gently through the pages of this book, you may be forgiven for thinking there are two types of drink that it covers. The fact is that whisky and whiskey are just different spellings of the same alcohol.

But on the other hand, they're not. Whisky comes from Scotland, while whiskey is made in the US and Ireland. Whisky can also be found in Canada, and when there's more than one of them, they're whiskies.

Meanwhile, when we talk about whisky in the generic sense, we use the Scottish spelling, no matter where it comes from. When we use the Scotch spelling, however, it can only come from Scotland.

Clear? Or just a little bit cloudy.

INTRODUCTION

Whisky is the most magical, most written about and discussed drink on the planet. For those who love it – and there are millions of us worldwide – the Gaelic meaning of the original word 'whisky' has a particular resonance: for the whisky devotee the amber nectar really is uisgebeatha – the water of life. Whisky is also the product that has put Scotland on the world map and with a level of influence and importance completely out of proportion to its size; Scotland is one of the great nations of the earth for the simple reason that nowhere else on earth can produce the range and quality of whiskies that Scotland produces. It is true that until the 1920s Ireland dominated the whisky export scene, but when the American market switched allegiance during Prohibition, Irish whiskey fell out of favour and has never regained its former dominating position.

Arguments still rage about whether the Scots or the Irish made whisky first – it's a pretty pointless debate given that ethnically the Irish and the Scots are the same people and that their early histories are intricately intertwined. The Scotti, from whom Scotland gets its name, was, for example, a Celtic tribe that left the Dublin area and settled in what is now Scotland long before Christianity came to these islands.

Over the centuries whisky has gathered around it great tales and great characters; tales of smuggling and wild escapades; tales of heroism, comedy and tragedy – and the best of those tales, anecdotes, quotations, legends, myths and mysteries are gathered here in a book that no one with the least interest in whisky can possibly afford to be without.

The Whisky Companion may not give you all the technical nuts and bolts about whisky production; it may not give you the most comprehensive statistics about brands and marketing, but it will bring you close to the essence of a unique spirit because, like this book, whisky is about pleasure; it's about the enjoyment of life.

Tom Quinn, Editor

WIT AND WHISKY

A drunk is up in court, and takes his place in front of the judge.

'You've been brought here for drinking whisky,' admonishes the judge.

'Okay,' says the drunk, 'let's get started.'

THE MAGNIFICENT SIX

The Classic Malts are some of the very best. Some authorities differ as to the exact make-up of the list – well, these things are a matter of taste – but the most accepted line-up is:

Cragganmore
Dalwhinnie
Glenkinchie
Lagavulin
Oban
Talisker

DRAM-ATIC WRITING

Tho' often baffled by the smugglers' ingenuity, the excisemen or gaugers as known in Scotland, sometimes had luck on their sides and proved quite as sharp as their opponents. During the afternoon of a bright summer day in 1825 when the scenic beauties of Liddendale were at their best, a mournful cortege draped in sombre trappings, moved slowly over the road leading from Newcastleton to the English border. A few days earlier a well-known smuggler had been drowned while unsuccessfully attempting to emulate young Lochinvar, by fording the Esk River where ford there was none and it was to carry through his interment that his friends were now accompanying the black plumed hearse to the place where the body of the deceased was lying.

All went well for several miles of the journey and the mourners were congratulating themselves on the early termination of their journey, when two arrogant and not over-polite excisemen riding up, commanded the procession to stop. One of them dismounted and in the face of loud protestations pulled out the coffin and prized up the lid. They found within 30 gallons of prime Scots whisky on its way across the border. The hearse and its driver went straight to Annan jail.

Weekly Scotsman, 13 June 1908

Scotland has traditionally been divided into four whisky-producing regions – Highland, Islay, Campbeltown and Lowland – with Speyside a modern and perhaps rather arbitrary subdivision of the Highlands. The Scottish Highlands can also be divided into North, South, East and West, but it is difficult to match these divisions to any differences in the taste of the various whiskies produced in the different areas.

One of the difficulties is that whiskies are almost always matured in old sherry or wine casks. Experts say that through the flavour imparted by maturation they can detect the peat and water flavours that reveal the region a whisky comes from. However, cynics are more doubtful, but there is no doubt that peat is an essential element in the final taste of a malt whisky. But what is peat?

Over thousands of years, decaying vegetation – mostly moss, heather, sedges and grasses, depending on a bog's location – created peat bogs up to 30 feet deep, but the exact nature of Scottish peat bogs also depended on a cold atmosphere, high rainfall, and poor soil drainage and aeration. The high rainfall causes waterlogging, which means the vegetation does not fully decay and the result is layer upon layer of rich black peat.

What is now seen as a special way to impart flavour to whisky was originally just a means to stop the barley germinating – once germination had taken place the process was halted by drying the barley over a peat fire; peat was used because it was the sole available fuel in a land where timber was scarce. Taste characteristics are also determined of course by the amount of peat used (sometimes very little or none) and by the peaty strength of the water.

Islay, the southernmost of the Inner Hebrides islands off the north-west coast and virtually a peat-sodden island, probably produces the strongest, peatiest malts of all; here, the local phrase that sums up the process of maturation is that time takes out the fire and leaves in the warmth. Whisky straight from the still is undrinkable and only years spent in an old sherry cask will allow the concoction to mellow into something unique.

Different barrels and casks will also add to the final result: American oak gives a delicate flavour; European oak creates a stronger headier flavour and in the cold damp warehouses where the whisky spends its early life, humidity causes the whisky to lose alcohol and to evaporate. The small quantity lost in this way is called 'the angels' share.'

CATCH OF A LIFETIME

A Victorian fisherman out spinning for salmon had caught nothing and evening was drawing in – he was particularly cross as it had been an expensive week at the best time of year, yet hardly a fish had shown.

The gillie rowed him across the river and he made what he knew would be his last cast. The spinner swung round in the deep pool and snagged tight on something apparently immovable. After pulling this way and that the fisherman thought he would simply have to break the line, but one last heave moved whatever it was that lay in the depths and up came a very old and decayed fisherman's canvas bag.

The fisherman was about to throw it back in disgust when he noticed the bag was still firmly closed – inside he found a beautiful silver reel and a large bottle of unopened whisky.

After such a catch, he said later, who cares about fish!

THE MOTHER TONGUE

The English corruption of Gaelic words, such as 'whisky' from 'uisge', can be seen in the name of Scotland's favourite malt, Glenmorangie. The name derives from the Gaelic words Gleann (Glen) mor (big) na (of) sith (peace). Glenmorangie can therefore be translated as 'Glen of Tranquillity'.

BEECHAM'S HOWLERS

The great conductor, eccentric and whisky enthusiast Sir Thomas Beecham, who founded Britain's Royal Philharmonic Orchestra in 1946, was once travelling in a non-smoking compartment on a train belonging to the Great Western Railway. No one knows for sure if he had enjoyed a dram or two of his favourite tipple before travelling, but his wit was unusually sharp that day.

A lady entered the compartment and proceeded to light a cigarette, saying: 'I'm sure you won't object if I smoke.'

'Not at all,' replied Beecham, 'provided that you don't object if I'm sick.'

'I don't think you know who I am,' the lady haughtily pointed out. 'I'm one of the directors' wives.'

'Madam,' said Beecham, 'if you were the director's only wife I should still be sick.'

DISTILLERY FOOTBALL

When sporting fanatic Robert Baxter moved to Belfast's Grosvenor Street in 1878, he quickly made friends with employees at the Royal Irish Distillery. By 1879, they'd formed the Distillery Cricket Club and then in 1880, the Distillery Football Club. The team began to play regularly on ground supplied by the owners of the distillery. In 1905, the team won the prestigious City Cup. They had moved several times, but were still fully supported by the distillery.

Distillery Football Club became one of Ireland's best-known football clubs. They travelled widely and eventually became the first Irish club ever to win a foreign match away from home: a 2-1 win over the English club Newton Heath, which was to become Manchester United. In European competition they drew in 1963 when playing against the Portuguese club Benfica.

But the early 1970s and the political unrest saw the destruction of the club's ground and most of its records. However, the club still survives today.

Distillery Football Club has never entirely lost its connection with the whisky trade that brought it into being – ironically, though, it outlasted the Royal Irish Distillery which went out of business more than half a century ago.

QUOTE UNQUOTE

*For a bad hangover take the juice of
two quarts of whisky.*
Eddie Condon, US jazz musician

WHISKY MYTHS

Bottles of whisky that resurface intact and (in theory) perfectly drinkable after decades hidden in some bricked-up cellar are always enthused about among whisky fans, but their enthusiasm has more to do with rarity than quality. One of the myths about whisky that even experts often fall for is that the older a whisky the better it is likely to taste. This is certainly true for some whiskies, but definitely not for all; like wine, only whiskies that are really good in the first place are likely to improve with age. The very best whiskies in the world having been left untouched maturing in their casks for half a century are said to float like pure spirit into the mouth, but those who've tasted less exalted but equally ancient whiskies often describe them as tasting of dead mouse, old cheese and diesel fuel!

AN OTHER COUNTRY

Whisky exports in litres per annum to countries beginning with 'An'

Andorra	818,208
Angola	179,882
Anguilla	15,218
Antigua and Barbuda	20,685

ARE YOU GETTING A HINT OF EEL?

Some of the more unusual flavours picked up by whisky reviewers:

Carbolic soap
Chestnut
Coconut
Eel
Fishy
Herbal
Juniper
Leaf mould
Peppery
Pine
Roasted
Salty
Seaweed

DRAM-ATIC WRITING

'My uncle's great journey was in the fall of the leaf, at which time he collected debts, and took orders, in the north; going from London to Edinburgh, from Edinburgh to Glasgow, from Glasgow back to Edinburgh, and thence to London by the smack. You are to understand that his second visit to Edinburgh was for his own pleasure. He used to go back for a week, just to look up his old friends; and what with breakfasting with this one, lunching with that, dining with the third, and supping with another, a pretty tight week he used to make of it. I don't know whether any of you, gentlemen, ever partook of a real substantial hospitable Scotch breakfast, and then went out to a slight lunch of a bushel of oysters, a dozen or so of bottled ale, and a noggin or two of whiskey to close up with. If you ever did, you will agree with me that it requires a pretty strong head to go out to dinner and supper afterwards.

Charles Dickens, *The Pickwick Papers*

HUNTIN', SHOOTIN', DRINKIN'

A Victorian sportsman who devoted his life to hunting, shooting and drinking whisky once challenged his gamekeeper to a shooting match in which both men had to shoot the new and hugely popular glass ball targets. These forerunners of the modern clay pigeon were heavy glass spheres filled with chicken feathers. They were thrown into the air from a spring-loaded trap and the shooter then had to break them in midair.

Neither the Victorian sportsman nor his gillie had much experience of shooting these new targets but the gamekeeper, a more practised shot, easily beat his employer who was furious. He demanded a return match and in order to ensure that he was the winner on this occasion he insisted that after each shot they must both drink a glass of whisky.

This time the sportsman won easily and commented: 'He has more experience of shooting. I have more experience of drinking whisky. I think that gave us an even handicap and the best man one – ie, me.'

The gamekeeper took three days to recover from the effects.

WHISKY WARFARE

In the trenches in France in 1914, tea, coffee, sugar, firewood and alcohol of any kind were very difficult to come by, but one or two ordinary soldiers became legendary for hunting around and finding essential items even when absolutely everyone else was convinced that local villages and farms had been absolutely stripped clean.

One private was so good at scrounging that his officers hated the idea of sending him into battle in case he was killed or injured. He was their top firewood, food and drink finder, and hardly a day passed when foraging behind the lines he didn't find something useful.

His status became almost godlike when he returned to his comrades one evening with a large bottle of unopened Scotch. Neither officers nor men could believe their eyes, particularly when the private began to return night after night with whisky, gin and sugar – and they were only a little disappointed when they discovered that their man had been stealing the whisky from his own side!

A report had gone round that items were disappearing from the senior officers and commanders' headquarters several miles back from the frontline trenches. The private's immediate superiors couldn't bring themselves to turn him in, but his job as chief forager was given to someone else from then on.

The whisky carousers – but where did the tradition of trying to touch the ceiling with your glass come from?

THE HARD STUFF

How was whisky tested for proof strength?
Answer on page 153.

EARLY IRISH

The earliest record for Irish distilling comes from the Red Book of Ossory, *compiled by an Irish bishop in the thirteenth or possibly the fourteenth century. Here we find an intriguing recipe for distilling aqua vitae from wine.*

Simple aqua vitae is to be made in the following manner: take choice one year old wine, and rather of a red than of a thick sort, strong and not sweet, and place it in a pot, closing the mouth well with a clepsydra made of wood, and having a linen cloth rolled round it; out of which pot there is to issue a cavalis leading to another vessel having a worm. This latter vessel is to be kept filled with cold water, frequently renewed when it grows warm and the water foams through the cavalis. The pot with the wine having been placed previously on the fire, distil it with a slow fire until you have from it one half of the quantity of wine that you put in.

The facts of whisky-making are deceptively simple:

You take some barley, soak it, let it germinate just a bit and then allow it to dry out again. In whisky parlance this is now malt. Some distilleries dry their barley using peat fires which gives their whisky a rich, smoky flavour. Next, the malt is ground up and deposited in a wooden vat or series of vats. Water is added and then the thick liquid is allowed to ferment until it becomes what is called wash (more often referred to as mash).

The vats are called washbacks and the yeasty smell of the fermenting mash is so strong that it can almost knock out the unwary – in fact it is pure CO_2, so strong that the air seems almost to burn the lungs.

The liquid wash is next piped to the vast copper stills that are so distinctive a feature of the whole whisky-making process. These giant beautifully rounded onion-shaped apparatuses are used to heat the mash. As the liquid evaporates, it rises through the long neck where it cools and condenses; it's then collected and recycled for another round of distillations (Scottish whisky is distilled twice, Irish whiskey three times). The spirit then goes to a glass-fronted box called the spirit safe. Finally, the distilled liquid is piped to wooden casks where, by law and custom, it waits for a minimum of three years – although usually much longer – before it can be drunk.

Of course this brief account leaves out of the equation the enormous skills involved in the various processes; the drying and germination of the barley has to be precise and only a practised eye is likely to get it right every time. The prowess of creating and maintaining the mash until it is just right for the distillation process is also critical and experience in this, as in so many whisky matters, is vital.

But even after the whisky has spent the requisite amount of time in the barrel, it still often has to be blended – and this is where a whole new range of skills is needed. For a start, each distillery has its own secret blend and these secrets are guarded jealously, because a distillery's reputation can rise or fall according to the quality of its blends and these can be very complex indeed. Different ages of whisky are used together with different types to create what the makers often call 'a whisky for every mood and occasion.'

Though the popularity of single malts is undiminished, the big money is in blends simply because the vast bulk of all whisky sold today is blended.

QUOTE UNQUOTE

Actually, it only takes one drink to get me loaded. Trouble is, I can't remember if it's the thirteenth or fourteenth.
George Burns, comedian

SOUND THE PART

Want to sound like a whisky buff? Swill the liquid in your glass, breathe heavily through one nostril, and pronounce that the whisky offers a combination of any three of the following adjectives. Smile graciously at the applause.

Argumentative
Cantankerous
Complex
Delectable
Ghostly
Heady
Iodine
Mystical
Overpowering
Peaty
Pleasing
Robust
Silky
Smooth

COPPER

It's a little-known fact that the copper from which whisky stills are made influences the flavour of the whisky. No research has been done on this, but it must be true since copper stills have a finite life of perhaps 25 to 30 years. As they age, they get thinner and thinner, but where is all that copper disappearing to?

The answer is that the copper gets into the water and from there into the whisky. This doesn't mean that whisky drinkers will gradually find their hair turning blue, but it does mean that subtle hints of copper flavour are almost certainly adding to the general magical and complex flavours that make up a good whisky.

Mind you, having said that, there is probably no real need for concern as according to one estimate, you would need almost 7,000 bottles of whisky to consume the equivalent of one euro-cent worth of copper!

18 *Number in millions of casks of whisky maturing in Scotland at any one time*

A TIP AND A NIP

A mohel – the official charged with the duty of circumcising young boys under the orthodox Jewish faith – follows many traditions. One of these is that he gives the child a small piece of cake soaked in whisky to suck just before (and during) what must be a very painful procedure.

Some mohels had a slight variation on this. First they would pour some whisky into their own mouth. Then after they had snipped off the skin at the end of the boy's penis, they would sterilise the wound by placing the penis in their mouth.

FLYING STEAM

When the first steam engines appeared, neither the public nor the specialists believed the right system had been hit upon. One whisky company – aware of the huge market of British soldiers in India – was intrigued by a 'patent aerial steam carriage to convey goods, and dispatches through the air, performing the journey between London and India in four days, and travelling at the rate of 75 to 100 miles per hour.'

Other bizarre transport systems based on steam appealed to all sorts of manufacturers. A copy of *The Globe* reported that a 'professional gentleman at Hammersmith has invented an entirely new system of railway goods carriage, which may be propelled without the aid of steam at an extraordinary speed, exceeding 60 miles an hour. This will be ideal for moving goods about the country.'

A Scottish distiller sang the praises of an invention put forward at a board meeting by Messrs Taylor and Couder. They had apparently patented an ingenious system by which a freight carriage was to be drawn along the line 'by the muscular power of the two guards who constantly accompany it. The system, which is at the present moment in use for towing purposes on many German rivers, the Elbe for one, required that an endless rope should be laid along the line, and wound on to a drum which was attached to the carriage, and made to revolve by force, whether it be manual or mechanical, supplied from inside the carriage itself.'

With whisky beginning to take the world by storm, many distillers were searching for a means to get their products across the world as fast and as cheaply as possible, and there is no doubt that the rapid development of the railway between 1830 and 1890 was key to the ultimate success of whisky as a Scottish export.

FOR PEAT'S SAKE

The Ardbeg distillery on the island of Islay, in western Scotland, used to have its own onsite maltings and was the last distillery on the island to produce all its own malt. The maltings were unusual in that there were no fans in the roof pagodas, so that the peat smoke permeated the malt for longer than at other distilleries, resulting in the distinctive and much admired peaty flavour of this single malt.

Ardbeg is, in fact, the most heavily peated of all Scotch whiskies, at 50+ parts per million (ppm) of phenols compared to very lightly peated malts which can be less than 2ppm. The maltings at the distillery are no longer used and the malt now comes from nearby Port Ellen.

WHISKY EATS

Scottish Whisky Fruit Cake, as recommended by www.scotchwhisky.net/cooking

175g currants, 175g sultanas, 110g glacé cherries (rinsed, dried, cut into halves), 75g mixed candied peel (finely chopped), 3tbsp whisky, 150g butter (room temperature), 150g soft brown sugar, 3 eggs (size 1), 225g plain flour, 1tsp baking powder, milk (if necessary), 2 level tbsp ground almonds, grated rind of 1 small orange, grated rind of 1 small lemon, 110g whole blanched almonds, $3^{1}/_{2}$tbsp single malt whisky (for feeding!), 18cm square or 20cm round cake tin, greased and lined with greaseproof paper. The night before: mix fruit, peel and 3tbsp whisky, cover and leave.

1. Pre-heat oven to gas mark 3, 325°F or 170°C.

2. Mix butter and sugar until light and fluffy, whisk in eggs slowly, fold in sifted flour and baking powder.

3. Mixture needs to be soft, dropping consistency; if too dry, add a tbsp of milk.

4. Carefully fold in ground almonds, the mix of currants, sultanas, cherries and peel, and orange and lemon rinds.

5. Spoon mixture into cake tin, smooth out, arrange whole blanched almonds on top.

6. Place cake in centre of oven for 2 to $2^{1}/_{2}$ hours.

7. Leave cake to cool in tin for 30 minutes, finish cooling on wire rack.

To feed the cake: weekly, make small holes in top and bottom of cake with darning needle and spoon tsps of whisky through holes. To store the cake: wrap in double greaseproof paper and store in foil or airtight container till needed.

FUNERAL TRAIN

In the early 1900s, whenever a stationmaster at Towcester, central England, died, the railway company put on a special train to carry the coffin and mourners to their ancestral home at the village of Slapton five miles away. The railway company also supplied 'a suitable supply of whisky' – two full cases!

The train waited at the nearest point to the church while bearers carried the coffin half a mile along a field path to the churchyard where the burial took place. The track was a single line so no other train could pass. At the station, railway officials drank a whisky farewell to their departed colleague.

The family were then conveyed back to Towcester. The train company, the Stratford-upon-Avon and Midland Junction Railway, was more than once in the receiver's hands, but it prided itself on giving a proper send-off to any staff who died while in service.

THE HARD STUFF

Which distillery has the only remaining traditional malt floor still in use in the Scottish Highlands?
Answer on page 153.

£1,000 A GLASS!

In May 2005, a British businessman paid £32,000 for one bottle of Dalmore 62 Single Highland malt. Only 12 bottles of the 62 were ever produced. All are in the hands of collectors and so far as anyone knows, none has been opened – they are just too valuable to be consumed. The anonymous businessman clearly thought this was rather silly, so having paid £32,000 for his bottle, he invited half a dozen friends to the hotel where he was staying and they drank the lot in just one evening – each glass was estimated to have cost more than £1,000!

The Dalmore 62 was blended from four now-vanished casks of single malt dating from 1868, 1876, 1926 and 1939, and each bottle has a unique hand-printed label and unique name. The bottle drunk in Surrey was called Matheson, after Alexander Matheson, the owner of the Dalmore Estate. Apparently whisky of this kind should be drunk with expensive coffee and – according to at least one master distiller – chocolate that is 86% cocoa mass!

WHISKY CURE

Recent research carried out by a group of doctors in Britain and the United States has revealed that malt whisky is a highly potent anti-cancer therapy. It appears that whisky contains high levels of an antioxidant that can kill cancer cells. According to the research, single malts contain more antioxidants than red wine.

Unfortunately, the research didn't mention the amount of whisky that would have to be drunk to make a difference, nor whether the damaging effects of the alcohol would outweigh the benefits!

QUOTE UNQUOTE

If you mean the demon drink that poisons the mind, pollutes the body, desecrates family life, and inflames sinners, then I'm against it. But if you mean the elixir of Christmas cheer, the shield against winter chill, the taxable potion that puts needed funds into public coffers to comfort little crippled children, then I'm for it. This is my position, and I will not compromise!
Anonymous US Congressman, speaking about whisky

BUT OFFICER, I JUST REALLY LOVE WHISKY

For many tourists, one of the best parts of a holiday is the duty-free booze you can get on the way home. And for those wanting to stock up on some whisky, here's how you can stay on the right side of the law if you're travelling in the EU.

There's no limit to the amount of excise goods (including alcohol) that you can buy in Europe, as long as they are carried by you and are for your own use. If you are bringing goods in to sell on then they are classed as being for a commercial purpose and can be seized.

Despite there being no limit to how much you can bring back, if you have several gallons of whisky in your suitcase, a customs officer will probably have their suspicions aroused and question you about what exactly you intend to do with so much whisky.

Guidelines state that you will be questioned if you exceed these quantities:

Coming in from the EU: 10 litres of spirits.

Coming in from outside the EU: 1 litre of spirits or strong liqueurs over 22% volume.

22 *Year in the nineteenth century when legal distilleries were allowed to operate at a reasonable licence fee*

HELP FROM KELP

In 1811, *The Statistical Account of Scotland* records show that barley formed roughly half the total of all crops grown in the Hebrides islands. Barley – or 'bere' as it was known locally – had the great advantage of ripening two or three weeks earlier than other cereals. It needed a growing season of just 10 to 15 weeks, and could grow on the poorest soil if kept well watered and fertilised with seaweed. Best of all, it made excellent whisky.

COCKTAILS THAT INCLUDE WHISKY AS THE MAIN INGREDIENT

False Whiskey Sour • Finger Me Good
Flaming D • Frozen Bird
Fuzzy Blue Gobbler • Golddigger
Hangover • Han Solo
I Love Rosa • Ink Street
Irish Catholic • Irish Hammer
Jim Morrison • Joe Cocker
J. R.'s Revenge • Kentucky Hot Tub
Klingon Disrupter • Left Hook
Little Leprechaun • Lloyd Special

GONE BUT NOTT FORGOTTEN

Des Walker is an English football player who is best known for being a long-serving defender at Nottingham Forest. He also played for England in the 1990 World Cup in Italy.

Walker started his career at Nottingham and stayed there for nine seasons before he was bought by top Italian club Sampdoria for the 1992/93 season. The Italian club paid the considerable sum of £1.5m for Walker. Sampdoria was at that time under the guidance of one Sven-Goran Eriksson.

But Walker was not able to settle at the club, despite its top-flight management and array of top international players. He made a swift return to English football the very next season, signing up with Sheffield Wednesday, who he stayed with for the next eight seasons.

Italy obviously didn't agree with Walker, although he did manage to pick up something while he was there – the nickname 'Johnny Walker Whisky'. Perhaps he was drowning his sorrows while he dreamt of Nottingham?

Lieutenant Colonel Alfred Daniel Wintle was born in 1897 in Russia where his father was employed as a diplomat. In spite of his Russian birth, or perhaps because of it, Wintle always claimed that he got down on his knees every night before he went to bed and thanked God for making him an Englishman. Being an Englishman was, he said: 'the highest responsibility as well as the greatest honour.'

He was besotted by the idea of Englishness and utterly biased against every other nation, but his European upbringing meant that he spoke German and French and was steeped in the culture of western and central Europe. Wintle believed that a proper regard for umbrellas and whisky was the true mark of a gentleman; both lay at the heart of the difference between an Englishman and a Frenchman or a German. 'The Frenchman gets up in the morning,' explained Wintle, 'and consults his barometer. If there is to be no rain, he leaves his umbrella at home, sallies forth and gets a drenching.' The Englishman, by contrast, is too stupid to understand all these barometers and things, so he always takes his umbrella with him. But it doesn't end there, for whatever the circumstances, 'no Englishman ever unfurls his umbrella, which means he gets wet.' No Englishman ever drinks effeminate beer. He drinks whisky.

As soon as World War I started Wintle joined up. On his first day in the trenches, the soldier next to him was killed instantly by a bullet to the head. Terrified, Wintle stood stock-still and then saluted. 'That did the trick,' he said later, 'and within thirty seconds I had again become an Englishman of action.' A few months later, he narrowly missed being killed when a shell blew him off his horse. He lost an eye and most of his left hand, but seemed more concerned about the welfare of his horse and relieved to hear that it was unharmed.

By 1938, Wintle was working in military intelligence and when the war started he made strenuous efforts to see active service, even though he was well into middle-age. He attempted to get to France by impersonating a senior officer and trying to steal an aeroplane. This led to a court martial, but Wintle was let off and sent to North Africa where he went with 'an unwavering determination to win and twenty cases of whisky.'

Wintle had once said that he'd like Schubert's 'Serenade' played at his funeral by the Royal Dragoons, one of the British army's oldest regiment, and his friend Cedric Mays had always said he would arrange it. But when Wintle died in 1966, the Dragoons were serving overseas. In a spirit that Wintle would have applauded, Mays fortified himself with the greater part of a bottle of Wintle's favourite whisky, went into the nave of Canterbury Cathedral, stood to attention and sang the whole thing on his own.

'I'll get at this whisky if it kills me!'
Or *why they invented the screw cap.*

DRAM-ATIC WRITING

It appears that in January 1816 William Phillmay and his wife Mary came before the justices. She'd been caught illegally distilling whisky in her house in the remote village of Kyle. Naturally enough she and her husband had objected to seeing the machinery by which their livelihood was earned, carted away. Straightaway the fiery cross was sent round and the clansmen, rallying to the summons, hastily pursued the retreating excise officers, overtaking them about one mile along the road.

Led by the Amazon Mary, armed with a poker of portentous size, a mob of some 20-strong fell upon the luckless excisemen and inflicted on them a most inhuman beating. Indeed so deadly was the onslaught that the officers were soon compelled to relinquish their capture and flee. The Phillmays' triumph was shortlived: she and her husband were sentenced to transportation for seven years for their share in the fight.

***Kilmarnock Standard,* November 1908**

QUOTE UNQUOTE

When we drink, we get drunk. When we get drunk, we fall asleep.
When we fall asleep, we commit no sin. When we commit no sin,
we go to heaven. Sooooo, let's all get drunk and go to heaven!
Brian O'Rourke

THE FINISHING TOUCH

Glenmorangie pioneered the launch of wood finishes in the 1990s. After maturation in ex-Bourbon casks, the spirit is transferred to different casks for a further period of maturation or 'finishing'.

Using casks that previously held port, sherry, Madeira or burgundy wines retains the essential balance of Glenmorangie, while adding new, intriguing characteristics.

Glenmorangie has experimented with various casks that previously held different wines or spirits for its Wood Finish range including:

Port • Fino Sherry
Oloroso Sherry
Madeira • Burgundy
Claret • Cognac
Côte De Nuits • Sauternes
Côte De Beaune • Malaga

A MOST UNUSUAL ADVERT

The Jewish diaspora included a small but substantial population of Jews who clung on in Morocco until the 1950s. Whisky has always been popular among Jews, both Orthodox and more secular, and in Morocco, special efforts were made by at least one whisky company to woo this particular market.

The Scottish distiller Lauder's, produced an eponymous whisky that was among its most successful exports. The company produced an advertisement for the Moroccan market for its famous export blend that had text in four languages: medieval Hebrew, modern Hebrew, French and Arabic, written in Hebrew characters. The main text appeared in Piyutim, a form of religious poem, associated with Jewish festivals. Piyutim were used in whisky advertisements because the North African Jewish community tradition was to drink whisky at births, weddings and other festivals. The adverts also pointed out that the whisky was, of course, kosher.

THE GOOD OLD DAYS

**Those wonderful years that saw the founding
of key Scottish distilleries.**

1751	Gilcomston
1775	Glenturret
1779	Bowmore
1786	Strathisla
1797	Glen Garioch
1798	Highland Park and Tobermory
1810	Glenburgie
1815	Laphroaig and Ardbeg
1816	Lagavulin
1817	Teaninich and Duntocher
1843	Glenmorangie

THINGS YOU SHOULD KNOW

Bruichladdich is Scotland's most westerly distillery.

Pulteney is the most northerly distillery in the Scottish Highlands.

Strathisla (1786) is the oldest malt whisky distillery in the Highlands.

Edradour is the smallest distillery in Scotland.

Glenfarclas make the strongest malt whisky legally available.

DRAM-ATIC WRITING

The journey down had been very tedious. After waiting for half an hour in the midnight turmoil of an August Friday in Waterloo station, they had seized an empty carriage, only to be followed by five north-countrymen, all of whom were affected by whisky. Olive, Helena, Louisa, occupied three corners of the carriage. The men were distributed between them. The three women were not alarmed. Their tipsy travelling companions promised to be tiresome, but they had a frank honesty of manner that placed them beyond suspicion. The train drew out westward. Helena began to count the miles that separated her from Siegmund. The north-countrymen began to be jolly: they talked loudly in their uncouth English; they sang the music-hall songs of the day; they furtively drank whisky. Through all this they were polite to the girls. As much could hardly be said in return of Olive and Louisa. They leaned forward whispering one to another. They sat back in their seats laughing, hiding their laughter by turning their backs on the men, who were a trifle disconcerted by this amusement.

DH Lawrence, *The Trespasser*

MEDICINE DRAM

Whisky has long been thought of as having restorative qualities: it was first drunk as a medicine, then rubbed on the skin like an ointment, splashed on the head to cure baldness, and given to women to help them conceive and to help them bear the pain of childbirth. It was, in short, thought of as a miracle liquid, hence the appellation *aqua vitae*. It was given to children and babies, sheep, lambs and pigs and even poured round the base of trees to give them a boost.

Such were its wondrous properties that some really did think it could restore life and, by tradition, at Irish wakes a dram would be pressed to the lips of the dead. Or maybe it was just to give them a final taste of the thing they most loved in life.

THE HARD STUFF

What percentage of the whisky market is made up by blends?
Answer on page 153.

ONE THAT GOT AWAY

Once, when spinning under the north shore, not far from a deep bay on a very famous salmon river, the owner of an equally famous distillery found he'd hooked the mother and father of all fish. It felt like a huge immovable rock and betrayed itself as a fish only by an occasional angry shake of the head that buzzed up the line.

Suddenly the fisherman's bait began, quietly, to move away.

A long fight ensued – so long in fact that the light began to fade and still the fish bored deep and stayed well out in the river seemingly unmoved by the pressure of a 20-pound breaking strain line.

After several hours, a huge head appeared out in the dark water and a great white mouth like that of a shark. When the fish was in the net at last, the fisherman was so astonished at its size – it must have weighed at least 40 pounds he later claimed – he simply stood and stared. The fish then seemed to convulse for a second and a miniature whisky bottle, its contents intact, popped out of the fish's mouth. The fisherman was so amazed that he forgot he had already unhooked the fish and with a giant thwack of its tail, it cleared the side of the net and disappeared once again into the deep water. All that was left was the small whisky bottle in a very large net.

'It wasn't even a good malt,' said the disgruntled fisherman to anyone who would listen back at his hotel.

A SLIPPERY QUESTION

Distilling produces a great deal of warm water; the question is, what do you do with it? Several Victorian distilleries found a most unusual answer, setting up eel-breeding areas in their warm-water outflows. The eel farms were highly profitable and the eels seemed unusually happy – perhaps because they were getting a whiff of the real thing!

STILL NOT LEGAL

Records from 1817 reveal the following illegal stills:

Alexander and John McFarlane, Auchnadryan, Largiesland

Hector and Finlay

Currie, Courshelloch, Largiesland

Donald McEachern, Auchnadryan, Largiesland

John Campbell, Carnbeg, Largiesland

Archibald McMurchy, Stewartfield, Clachan

Samuel and Coll McAlester & Co Brantian, Ballochroy Glen

Donald McMillan & Neil McEachern, Achravad, Clachan

John McFiggan, farmer, Barr

David Turner, innkeeper, Barr

Neil McCorkindale and Edward McCallum, Barr Glen

Gilbert McEachern and Angus Bell, Clachaig Glen, Muasdale

Archibald McEachern, Cleongart, Bellochantuy

Neil Downie and Malcolm Curry, Drumore-na-Bodach

Some 20 other individuals and families in Rhunahaorine shared in a still hidden in a tunnel in a nearby peat bog.

WASTED CROPS

In the seventeenth and eighteenth centuries, a huge amount of the barley grown in Scotland was wasted because of the way it was used for distilling. Because whisky-making was illegal, there were no permanent floors to lay out the barley to germinate. Instead the grain was spread out across shallow ponds and puddles before being spread out on muddy fields, or in bothies or caves, to germinate. Much of it inevitably went bad, but the pleasure to be gained from whisky made such losses worth while it seems, despite the fact that the barley was arguably far more useful as a food substance.

The *Marie Celeste* is, of course, the most famous of all ghost ships, but she is by no means the only one – many other ships have vanished only to be discovered years later, still seaworthy, yet entirely unmanned. Even when there is no real reason to think that some kind of malevolent supernatural influence is at work, the discovery of a floating hulk with all its gear more or less intact and yet not a man aboard is enough to make the most convinced sceptic nervous. A British naval ship cruising the coastline of Chile in 1913 made a discovery that the captain of the ship never forgot; it is said that long after he'd retired he still thought of the discovery with a cold shudder.

His ship had been on the look-out for suspicious trading vessels that might be involved in smuggling or worse, when the lookout spotted a large sailing cargo ship moving slowly but under full sail. Her sails were tattered and filthy but they were by no means ineffective. And though she seemed weather-beaten, her condition was certainly not enough to arouse more than a mild suspicion that this ragged craft might be up to no good.

The captain of the British naval ship decided, almost as a matter of routine, to investigate, but he expected to find nothing more than the usual band of harmless South American sailors aboard. He asked the helmsman to get close to the sailing ship. After several attempts to make contact using various signals, the baffled captain gave the order to board. Three men swung over the treacherous sea to the strange sailing ship, but returned as quickly as they'd gone, their faces telling the captain that something was dreadfully amiss. By this time other members of the Navy ship's crew had noticed a number of curious things about the sailing ship – her masts and sails, for example, were covered in a thick green moss-like substance and wherever they looked along her deck they could see no sign of life. The crew could have all been below deck, but a sailing ship needs continual work to keep her on course and that work has to be carried out on deck, so the apparent absence of human life was odd indeed.

The captain ordered a boarding party back onto the sailing ship and this time they searched more carefully. They discovered the skeleton of a man lying beneath the helm; a dozen more skeletons were found in the forward hold and seven on the ship's bridge. There were no signs of violence or of a struggle. Each skeleton was dressed in the tattered rags that had once been clothes and strewn everywhere were whisky bottles, most of them still full or only partly empty. It was only when the boarding party cleared the green slime from the side of the sailing ship's prow that they could make out her name – the *Marlborough Glasgow*. Safely back in port the captain of the naval vessel was able to uncover her strange story.

The *Marlborough Glasgow* had left the port of Littleton in New Zealand more than 20 years earlier, in 1890. She had a crew of 23 and was carrying a cargo of wool and mutton. Captain Hird was in command. The ship should have arrived back in port a few weeks later, but was never heard of again – at least that is until 1913. Search parties went out to look for her towards the end of 1890, but nothing was found and it was assumed she'd been lost in a storm with all hands.

Her discovery in 1913 caused a sensation, but how she managed to drift for 23 years without being overwhelmed by storms and driven onto rocks or sandbanks is a mystery that will never be solved. Tests on the crew revealed nothing about how they died, but the fact that they lay in groups together suggests that whatever overwhelmed them did so incredibly quickly.

IT'S THE WHISKY TALKING

Whisky was traditionally only drunk by what the Victorians would have called 'forward gels' [girls].

QUOTE UNQUOTE

Always remember that I have taken more out of alcohol
than alcohol has taken out of me.
Winston Churchill, politician

DRAM-ATIC WRITING

'That drove the spigot out of him!' cried Stubb. "Tis July's immortal Fourth; all fountains must run wine today! Would now, it were old Orleans whiskey, or old Ohio, or unspeakable old Monongahela! Then, Tashtego, lad, I'd have ye hold a canakin to the jet, and we'd drink round it! Yea, verily, hearts alive, we'd brew choice punch in the spread of his spout-hole there, and from that live punch-bowl quaff the living stuff.'

Herman Melville, *Moby Dick*

INGREDIENTS FOR SUCCESS

Bannockburn

A dram of Scotch whisky
A dash of Worcester sauce
A dash of tomato juice
A slice of lemon
Ice

BRUNEL IN SEARCH OF A PINT (OF WHISKY)

The Quaker director gave a great breakfast to celebrate the opening of one of the railway lines with which the great Isambard Kingdom Brunel was connected. But there was a problem: the Quakers hated alcohol and Brunel loved it, particularly whisky. The director was in fact a strict teetotaller.

The breakfast went well enough until Brunel asked for a drink. He always drank with his breakfast and famously said he 'could not make a breakfast on pines, grapes and coffee.'

'I cannot breakfast at this hour without something of the kind,' said Brunel. 'I must help myself, and return to finish your good things.'

Followed by two or three of the party, he left the Quaker's banquet, found a pub nearby, enjoyed several glasses of his favourite malt and then rejoined the Quaker breakfast.

32 *Age of Macallan single Highland malt Scotch whisky that now costs more than £600 per bottle*

REPELS GRAVEL

**In 1577, English chronicler Raphael Holinshed records
the virtues of whisky:**

Being moderately taken,
it slows the age,
it cuts phlegm,
it lightens the mind,
it quickens the spirit,
it cures the dropsy,
it heals the strangulation,
it pounces the stone,
its repels gravel,
it pulls away ventositie,
it keeps and preserves the head
from whirling,
the eyes from dazzling,
the tongue from lisping,
the mouth from snuffling,
the teeth from chattering,
the throat from rattling,
the weasan from stiffing,
the stomach from womblying,
the heart from swelling,
the belly from wincing,
the guts from rumbling,
the hands from shivering,
the sinews from shrinking,
the veins from crumpling,
the bones from aching,
the marrow from soaking,
and truly it is a
sovereign liquor
if it be orderly taken.

THINGS YOU SHOULD KNOW

Jameson's is the biggest-selling Irish whiskey outside Ireland.

Cooley is the only Irish-owned Irish distillery in the world.

Aberfeldy is the most popular Scotch in America.

Japanese maker Suntory has the largest still in the world.

The world's largest-selling Scotch whisky is Johnnie Walker Red Label.

DANES DISTIL

Scandinavia's love affair with whisky reached something of a peak when Danish liquor company CLOC installed whisky-making equipment at their factory in 1949. They got barley, peat and pure local water to try to create a unique Danish version of the famous Celtic drink.

When the first batch was made it was carefully stored in barrels and left for the requisite three years – just as 'real' Scottish whisky is always left.

The whisky was available for tasting by September 1952, but it was ruinously expensive at £2 a bottle. Despite the high price, the CLOC distillery continued to make the spirit until as recently as 1974 – their biggest problem was simply that most people preferred whisky imported from Scotland and Ireland.

WHISKY THE CLEANER

Whisky has been used as an excellent (if expensive) polishing agent to make the following shine:

Brass
Copper
Diamonds
Formica
Glass
Gold
Silver

JUST A QUICK ONE

It took nearly three years for regular train commuters on the main lines out of nineteenth-century London to become aware of something slightly odd. When rumours spread and an investigation had been set up by the railway companies, the pieces of a puzzle quickly came together to uncover a bizarre confidence trick.

One evening, two and half years earlier, just as a commuter train was about to leave Euston station, a well-spoken young man was seen running along the platform shouting up at passengers through the open windows: 'A woman has fainted; does anyone have any whisky?'

Invariably – this being the 1890s – someone would have a hip-flask of whisky and it would be handed down. 'That's terribly kind. I'll just go and administer a dose and be right back.'

The young man dashed back along the platform like some latter-day Sir Galahad. But the elderly gentleman who'd handed over his hip-flask waited in vain

for it to be returned. He spoke to the guard and the ticket collector. Neither knew a thing about a woman fainting.

Over the following months, the same or a similar trick was carried out on trains about to leave King's Cross, Liverpool Street, Victoria and Waterloo stations. The young man escaped detection because he carried out his little deception only once every two weeks and each time at a different station. But then he became over-confident and his hit rate increased to once, sometimes even twice a week.

He was finally arrested when a passenger remembered a similar earlier incident – the passenger reported his suspicions to the guard who collared the young man as he headed towards the station entrance. The police later found 30 silver flasks at the young man's home – all empty. During his interrogation by the police he confessed that the flasks were of no interest to him – it was the whisky he was after!

AQUA VITAE

In his Description of Pembrokeshire *published in 1603,*
George Owen of Henllys writes:

As many out of the county of Wexford say they understand no Irish, neither do any well understand his English. They are so increased that there are some whole parishes inhabited by the Irish, having not one English or Welsh but the parson of the parish. And these Irish people here do use their country trade in making of aquavitie in great abundance which they carry to be sold abroad the country on horseback and otherwise, so that weekly you may be sure to have aquavitie to be sold at your door, and by means thereof it is grown to be a usual drink in most men's houses instead of wine, some of them making exceeding good, and sold better cheap than in any part of England or Ireland, for I have drunk as good as some rosa solis made by them, and this sold usually for 17d. a quart, but commonly you shall have very good for 10d. or 12d. the quart, which is better cheap than ever I could buy the like in any part of England.

QUOTE UNQUOTE

The problem with the world is that
everyone is a few drinks behind.
Humphrey Bogart, actor

WHISKY MYTHS

It is said that the Irish writer Brendan Behan drank a whole bottle of whisky (or its equivalent) every day for more than a decade. Even allowing for a little exaggeration it is certainly true that Behan was a legendary drinker, but he would have been the first to admit that though in small quantities whisky helped him write, it was not so good when taken to excess. It was perhaps a symptom of his attention-seeking or desire to shock, or even of the onset of delirium tremens, that when he was deep in his cups Behan would often rush into hotels, libraries and TV studios and immediately remove his trousers. Behan's life and love of whisky and other strong drink certainly gives the lie to the old myth that alcohol is good for summoning the creative muse!

For Behan, Dylan Thomas, Hemingway and other whisky lovers, an early love of whisky certainly did help them write, but drinking too much eventually took their talent away – for good.

LUCKY BEGGARS

Number of people employed in the whisky industry in 1994, the 500th anniversary of Scottish malt:

Highland Region	485
Grampian Region	1,605
Strathclyde Region	6,753
Lothian Region	1,761
Tayside and Dumfries and Galloway Regions	653
Rest of UK	386
Total	**13,804**

THE LEGEND OF LIVET

Speyside has long been famous for its distilleries, but during the inter-war years most of them decided to adopt the additional name Glenlivet – the name comes from a small glen on Speyside. Whiskies from this part of the Highlands have been renowned since the eighteenth century when they were all illegal, and such is the pull of the notoriety of Glenlivet that by the beginning of the twenty-first century more than half of all Scotland's malt whisky distilleries were based in this small corner of the Highlands.

THE PAGODA ROOF

The distinctive pagoda-style roof that typifies the Scottish distillery can be traced largely to one man, the greatest of all distillery architects: Charles Cree Doig, who was born in Linrathen, Angus, in 1855.

Brilliant at maths, Doig left school in 1870 and joined an architect's office. He married and moved to Elgin in 1882 where he worked for a land surveyor. By 1908 he was running the business and had changed its name to Doig and Sons. In the intervening period, his firm had become famous for its work on distilleries – Doig and Sons built or rebuilt more than 100, right across the region. The most distinctive feature was the curved-sided pagoda ventilation tower, the original design drawings for which still survive in Doig's hand.

Charles Doig's obituary published after his death in 1918 says it all: 'Additions and reconstructions were extensively undertaken by many distillers of Highland malt whisky, and in all this work the services of Mr Doig as an architect were very much in demand. All over Scotland and in the north of Ireland his work was well known, and in the course of his professional career he formed many warm friendships among the distillers.'

36 *Number of months that John Begg Blue Cap Scotch is aged in Scotland before being blended and bottled in the US*

SIGNIFICANT EVENTS

1816 Sikes hydrometer adopted for testing alcoholic content

1826 Robert Stein invents continuous still

1913 Teacher's introduce a new cork

1959 Whisky rationing comes to an end – probably the most significant event of them all

THE HARD STUFF

What is the word used to describe the mixing
of malt and grain whiskies?
Answer on page 153.

DRAM-ATIC WRITING

There's a brave little bark stealing out in the dark,
From her nest in the bristling bay;
The fresh breeze meets her dingy sheets,
And swiftly she darts away;
She never must run
in the eyes of the sun,
But along with the owl take wing,
She must keep her flight for the moonlight night,
For she carries the Smuggler King.
A monarch is he as proud as can be
Of a strong and mighty band,
The bullet and blast may go whistling past,
But he quails neither heart nor hand.
He lives and dies with his fearful prize
Like a hunted wolf he'll spring,
With trigger and dirk, to the deadliest work,
And fight like a Smuggler King.
Back from the wave,
To his home in the cave,
In the sheen of the torches' glare;
He reigns the lord of a freebooter's board,
And never was costlier fare.
Right firm and true were the hearts of the crew,
There's faith in the shouts that ring
As they stave the cask, and drain the flask,
And drink to the Smuggler King.

Anon

When Ireland was awash with distilleries – well over 1,000 at one point in the eighteenth century – a young entrepreneur called Peter Roe bought a small distillery on Dublin's Thomas Street. What made this distillery unusual was that it was run entirely by a windmill – in fact Roe's windmill was said to be the biggest smock windmill in the world. Though the distillery is long gone, the tower of the old windmill – now known as St Patrick's Tower – still stands, a rocky landmark amid the urban landscape.

Two years after Roe started distilling, Arthur Guinness set his Brewery – the St James's Gate Brewery – directly opposite Roe's premises. The two men almost immediately fell out and their feud was to last for years. Guinness claimed his porter (as Guinness was popularly known in Ireland) was the nurse of the people, while Roe's whiskey and, by implication, all other whiskies, was the curse of the people.

By 1766, the Roe family had established another distillery on nearby Pimlico Street. The Thomas Street and Pimlico Street distilleries were later combined to create George Roe & Company which, by 1887, had become the biggest distillery in the world outside the USA. The company produced more than two million gallons of

whiskey a year. The Roe family used their immense profits for the public good – paying for the restoration of Dublin's Christ Church Cathedral, for example. When a new road was cut through the district it was officially named Lord Edmund Street, but known locally always as Roe Row.

In 1889, the Jameson Distillery and Roe Distillery joined forces to create the Dublin Distilling Company, but by the early years of the twentieth century the once world-dominating company was in trouble. The rebellion against British rule culminating in the Easter Rising of 1916 made trading difficult for the distiller and by 1926, Roe & Co had vanished. At last, the 200-year-old feud between Guinness and Roe & Co ended in victory for the brewer, when the old site of the distillery was taken over by Guinness.

As with so many long-gone distilleries, stocks of Roe's whiskey lasted for many years after the company stopped manufacturing and every now and then a case or an odd bottle turns up. In the 1980s, several cases were found in the sealed basement of a house in Dublin and after so many decades of storage in near-perfect cellar conditions – damp and cold and undisturbed – the 80-year-old bottles of Roe's finest were said to be a taste of heaven'.

'*I can fly! I can fly!*'
Pure malt brings table-top antics.

QUOTE UNQUOTE

Anybody who hates dogs and loves whiskey can't be all bad.
WC Fields, comedian and whisky aficionado

DUTY CALLS

During World War I, the Argyll and Sutherland Highlanders were billeted at the Glenmorangie Distillery in Tain. The malt barns were converted into makeshift barracks for the duration of the summer of 1915 and every summer for the remainder of the war, the troops would make the malts barns their base. The barns were perfect for the purpose as they offered plenty of room and the nearby Tarlogie Springs (the unique, mineral-rich water source used for Glenmorangie) were on hand to provide a fresh water supply. Presumably there was also a good supply of another kind of liquid. However, we can only speculate as records of any consumption of the local speciality have sadly not survived!

WILY CELTS

After the 1707 Act of Union, which brought together the English and Scottish parliaments, English tax officials crossed the border in droves confident they could bring the illegal distillers to heel. They never really succeeded and were constantly outwitted by the wily Celts. A century later, the excise laws were so confused that no two distilleries were taxed at the same rate and illegal distilleries still outnumbered legal set-ups.

COCKTAILS THAT INCLUDE WHISKY AS THE MAIN INGREDIENT

McTavish
Menace Shot
M.J.A.
Modern Cocktail
Modified Duck Fart
Mowed Lawn
Ma Bonnie Wee Hen
Nuclear Rainbow
Pablo's Shot
Peach Smoothie
Pio's Beating Stick
Protein Smoothie
Purple Lobster

CASTING AT THE SAVOY

Two Americans staying in London in the early 1950s had an argument over whether or not it would be possible to cast a fly from the roof of their hotel – the Savoy – over the gardens and the busy Embankment and into the Thames.

They were so determined to settle the dispute that they went along to Hardy Brothers, the tackle-makers, and asked them to decide if such a thing was possible. Hardy Brothers approached Esmond Drury who agreed to attempt the feat in return for a case of the finest whisky the Americans could afford. Next day, Drury was tied securely to a chimney on the hotel roof.

With the help of a policeman who stopped all the traffic on the Embankment, Drury proved that it was indeed possible to cast a fly into the Thames from the roof of the Savoy – and he went home with a case of some of Britain's most expensive booze!

WORLD'S OLDEST MALT

The last bottle of the world's oldest single malt whisky – Glenfiddich Rare Collection 1937 – was sold by the family-owned Glenfiddich Distillery in Speyside to the duty-free department of Hong Kong's Chek Lap Kok Airport for 'around £10,000'. The distillery says the whisky is the oldest single malt whisky in the world as it was left to mature in a single cask for 64 years.

Glenfiddich malt master David Stewart declared: 'On the one hand, we're extremely proud of having produced a whisky of such a fantastic quality that's stood the test of time and on the other, there's a tinge of sadness at saying goodbye to the last bottle.'

INGREDIENTS FOR SUCCESS

Whisper

A dram of Scotch
A dash of French Vermouth
A dash of Italian Vermouth
Cracked ice

Clansman's Coffee

A dram of Scotch
A dash of Sambucca
Black coffee
Whipped cream

MEDIEVAL MIKE

Michael Scot is one of the most remarkable medieval Scots. He was born in the Borders Region in the 1170s, was educated in Oxford and Paris, visited Bologna (in 1220), and Palermo, where he was court astrologer to Frederick II.

Scot was a widely read scientist and a number of medieval manuscripts suggest that he knew the art of distilling what he called *aqua ardens* or *aqua vitae*.

The difficulty is that the manuscripts that refer to Scot were compiled several centuries after he is thought to have died in the 1220s. But the fact remains that distilling may well have reached Scotland in the 1200s long before the first official mention of distilled spirit some 200 years later.

WRECKED

On 12 January 1816, while two excisemen were searching for smuggled whisky in the neighbourhood of Cruff, they encountered a band of 28 Irishmen carrying between them 140 gallons of whisky in bladders. The excisemen told the Irishmen to hand over their bladders. Instead, the Irishmen put them all in a heap, around which they formed in circular array and with bludgeons and pistols ready, dared the officers to come and take the prize. Wisely the excisemen retired with what dignity they could amid the jeers of the smugglers.

DRAM-ATIC WRITING

When the men met in the morning they were supposed to have breakfasted at home, and perhaps had had their private dram, it being cold work in a dark wintry dawn, to start over the moor for a walk of some miles to end in standing up to the knees in water; yet on collecting, whisky was always handed round; a lad with a small cask – a quarter anker – on his back, and a horn cup in his hand that held a gill, appeared three times a day among them. They all took their 'morning' raw, undiluted and without accompaniment, so they did the gill at parting when the work was done; but the noontide dram was part of a meal. There was a twenty minutes' rest from labour, and a bannock and a bit of cheese taken out of every pocket to be eaten leisurely with the whisky... Sometimes a floater's wife or bairn would come with a message; such messenger was always offered whisky. Aunt Mary had a story that one day a woman with a child in her arms, and another bit thing at her knee, came up among them; the horn cup was duly handed to her, she took a 'gey guid drap' herself, and then gave a little to each of the babies. 'My goodness, child,' said my mother to the wee thing that was trotting by the mother's side, 'doesn't it bite you?' 'Ay, but I like the bite,' replied the creature.

A large bothy was built for them at the mouth of the Druie in a fashion that suited themselves; a fire on a stone hearth in the middle of the floor, a hole in the very centre of the roof just over it where some of the smoke got out, heather spread on the ground, no window, and there, after their hard day's work, they lay down for the night, in their wet clothes – for they had been perhaps hours in the river – each man's feet to the fire, each man's plaid round his chest, a circle of weary bodies half stupefied with whisky, enveloped in a cloud of steam and smoke, and sleeping soundly till the morning.

Elizabeth Grant, *Memoirs of a Highland Lady*, 1898

TANTALISING TALIESIN

The great Welsh poet Taliesin (who died in the sixth century) mentions the distilling of mead in his *Mead Song*. Taliesin was the court poet for Urien, who ruled Rheged, one of the great kingdoms of north England. Nennius, the ninth-century Celtic historian, tells us in his *Historia Brittonum*, that Taliesin was one of the greatest of all bardic poets.

The Book of Taliesin, which survives only in manuscript from the fourteenth century, gives a tantalising if ambiguous account of mead-making and drinking that suggests that the kind of mead drunk in Wales during the Dark Ages might well have been distilled thus creating the earliest known whisky. If this is correct then Taliesin's whisky would almost certainly have been sweeter than modern whiskies since the basic ingredient of mead is honey.

NUMBER-CRUNCHING

3 – number of years a Scottish whisky must be matured or stored in Scotland before it can legally be called whisky

12 – number of years whisky would normally mature to achieve optimum taste

40 – number of different whiskies used to create Dewar's White Label

199 – number of distilleries in operation in 1900

WIT AND WHISKY

On reaching his plane seat, a man is surprised to see a parrot strapped in next to him. He asks the stewardess for a coffee whereupon the parrot squawks: 'And get me a whisky, you cow!'

The stewardess, flustered, brings back a whisky for the parrot and forgets the coffee. When this omission is pointed out to her, the parrot drains its glass and bawls: 'And get me another whisky, you silly moo!'

Quite upset, the girl comes back shaking with another whisky, but still no coffee. Unaccustomed to such slackness the man tries the parrot's approach. 'I've asked you twice for a coffee! Go and get it now or I'll kick your sorry behind!'

The next moment both he and the parrot have been wrenched up and thrown out of the emergency exit by two burly stewards. Plunging downwards the parrot turns to the man and says: 'For someone who can't fly, you've got a lot of lip!'

NICE LITTLE EARNER

Whisky is the UK's fifth best export earner.

HOW TO DRINK WHISKY

Experts say you should drink whisky:

At room temperature
With water if it's at cask strength
With ice to reduce dominant flavours
When you are in a good mood
When you are in a bad mood
When you are sad
When you are happy
All states in between!

THE WRONG END OF THE STICK

In his *A Tour of Scotland and the Western Isles* published in 1772, Thomas Pennant wrote that 'despite the quantity of bere [ie barley] raised, there was a dearth, the inhabitants of Kintyre being mad enough to convert their bread into poison, distilling annually six thousand bolls of grain into whisky.'

FRONGOCH

At the turn of the twentieth century, Wales was a whisky-producing nation. However, with the demise of the Frongoch distillery, Britain's third great Celtic nation ceased to be a whisky producer. No one alive today can remember the taste of Frongoch whisky, but the Welsh never quite gave up the idea of producing their own amber nectar. In the early 1970s, the dream became a reality – OK so the new 'chwisgi' as it was called in Welsh was based on imported Scottish whisky, but the added ingredients were designed to give the new drink a distinct Welsh flavour.

The man behind the new Welsh chwisgi was Dafydd Gittins who set up shop in the Brecon Beacons and began marketing a blend Swn Y Mor (Welsh for 'sound of the sea'). Swn Y Mor was a blend of Scottish-distilled malt whisky and Welsh-distilled grain spirit, but rumours began to spread that there was something odd about this as – so far as anyone knew – no Welsh distillery was operating at the time and the origins of the Welsh spirit seemed at the very least, rather mysterious.

WHISKY MYTHS

Irish legends mention a fearsome drink that was brewed by the gods of the underworld. The drink is never explicitly named but it was said to drive men wild. According to the way in which it was brewed, it could make a man have hallucinations or give him the strength of '40 giants'. Yet other variations on the mystery brew were said to be able to turn a man into a horse or a goat. But if the gods of the underworld decided that a warrior was a good fellow – or even if they just decided they disliked a particular warrior's enemy more than they disliked him – they would brew a drink that made the warrior invincible, not to mention turning him into a great – and inexhaustible – lover!

Some sort of distilled liquor may well have been on the minds of those who told these ancient stories, but one suspects that it would have tasted very different from the whisky we know today.

THE INTERNATIONAL SPIRITS CHALLENGE – RECENT GLENMORANGIE MEDALLISTS

2003 Silver – Glenmorangie 25 Years Old
2004 Bronze – Glenmorangie Madeira Matured
2005 Silver – Glenmorangie 30 Years Old Oloroso Finish
2005 Bronze – Glenmorangie Artisan Cask

DRAM-ATIC WRITING

'It is impossible,' declared Lord Holland in a speech before the House of Lords, 9 July, 1805, 'totally to prevent whisky smuggling; all that the legislature can do is to compromise with a crime which, whatever laws may be made to constitute it a high offence, the mind of man can never conceive as at all equalling in turpitude those acts which are breaches of clear moral virtues.' Adam Smith in his famous definition of a smuggler as 'a person who, though no doubt highly blamable for violating the laws of his country, is frequently incapable of violating those of natural justice and who would have been in every respect an excellent citizen had not the laws of his country made that a crime which Nature never meant to be so,' states the defence for whisky smuggling with an even greater directness.

Athol Forbes, *The Romance of Smuggling*

IT'S THE WHISKY TALKING

Even the best whisky in the world can't cheer some people up!

QUOTE UNQUOTE

Give an Irishman lager for a month, and he's a dead man. An Irishman is lined with copper, and the beer corrodes it. But whiskey polishes the copper and is the saving of him.
Mark Twain, writer

MUSIC TO THE EARS

Blood or Whiskey: A six-piece Irish punk band from Kildare and Dublin. Described by *Rolling Stone* as 'slightly demented yet oddly charming'.

Whiskey in the Jar: An Irish folk group based in Manchester.

The Whiskey Cats: A white funk band who throw a sound and light spectacular.

The Whiskey Priests: A five-piece group formed by brothers Gary and Glenn Miller (no, not that one). In 20 years, they've already got over 1,000 live performances under their cassocks.

VISITING THE WORKS

Alfred Barnard remembers a visit to the Islay distillery at Perth in his book The Whisky Distilleries of the United Kingdom.

We found the Distillery... about 300 yards from the bridge, and planted on the front of a hill facing the Tay. It consists of a series of stone buildings erected round a quadrangle, covering one and a half acres of ground. Under the guidance of the manager we commenced our tour of inspection from the upper roadway at the back of the works, where we found ourselves on a level with the Granary Floors, two in number.

In the floor at the end of each of these, there are circular openings through which the barley is dropped into the Steeps below. Descending a staircase we reached the Malt Barns... The Steeps are composed of brick and cement, but the floor is made with a composition, which, although hard, is slightly moist, thus enabling the Distiller to malt all the year round... We ascended by an outside stone staircase to the Kiln Floor... The building is 22 feet square; peat only being used in the drying... we proceeded to inspect the Malt Stores, which consist of three separate enclosed Malt Deposits, where the malt is kept from the air and light as much as possible. From this department we crossed a timber bridge over the quadrangle, into the Mill, which contains a pair of metal rollers and usual machinery; from thence we went through the Grist Loft, where there is a Hopper for feeding a Steel's Mashing Machine, and also two Heating Tanks, holding together 3,500 gallons.

Afterwards we passed to the Mash House, an apartment 50 feet square, with paved Boor. It contains a Mash-tun 13 feet in diameter and 5 feet deep, stirred with oars, and an Underback of similar proportions. Leaving this house for a few minutes we entered the Tun Room, where there are four Washbacks, each with a capacity of 4,000 gallons; and over the roof, a set of open coolers with a revolving fan therein. The worts, before running into these Coolers, pass through a Drum Refrigerator... We noticed a small chamber, wherein is placed the Wash Charger holding 8,000 gallons.

Retracing our steps we came to the Still House, where there are four Pot Stills, two of them Wash Stills, holding 700 gallons; the others, Spirit Stills, holding 600 and 350 gallons respectively. At the back of these Stills are three Worm Tubs, supplied with water from a small stream, which runs through the Distillery, and is used for no other purpose. The water from the Tay is used for brewing, and is pumped up from the river to a cistern at the highest point of the works. Following our guide we inspected the Receiver Room, containing a Low-wines Receiver, 500 gallons; feints Receiver, 500 gallons; and a Spirit Receiver, 700 gallons; also the Spirit Safe... The annual output is 30,000 gallons.

The Swedes and the Danes have had a long love affair with spirits of one kind or another – their own aquavit, a kind of vodka, has its origins in the Viking past, but more recently the Scandinavians have developed a great love of another spirit – whisky. Thus it was that in 1955 in the Swedish town of Södertälje, a second-hand set triple-still set from the Scottish Lowland distillery of Bladnoch was re-erected. The Swedes were in business.

The first batch of whisky from the Swedish distillery was left to mature for six years and then marketed as 'Skeppet' (Ship). It was a blend made from 45% of the Södertälje single malt and 55% grain whisky from the Åhus distillery in the southern province of Skåne, home of Absolut vodka.

The Swedes searched high and low across their country for the right ingredients – barley for the single malt had come from the province of Skåne, the peat from Småland and water from the nearest tap! They bought in used sherry butts in the best Scottish tradition. For 11 years the distillery worked well and produced something in the region of one million litres of whisky. When the distillery finally closed in 1966 some of its equipment was transferred to Stockholm's Wine and Spirit Museum. The stills were sold to Ödåkra in Skåne where they are still in use producing alcohol for aquavits.

THE HARD STUFF

What is the strength of Scotch whisky sold
(a) in the UK, (b) overseas?
Answers on page 153.

THIS B TRUE

Ball of malt – The term for a glass of whiskey in Ireland.

Beading – An inaccurate way of judging the alcoholic strength of a whisky. When a bottle is shaken, small bubbles will form. The bigger the bubbles and the longer they last, the greater the alcoholic strength of the spirit.

Bond – Warehouses in which whisky is stored until excise duty has been paid.

Bourbon – A whisky produced in the United States made from a mash of a minimum 51% corn, distilled to a maximum strength of 80% ABV (ie 160 proof) and put into new charred oak barrels at 62.5% ABV.

I feel sorry for people who don't drink. When they wake up in the morning, that's as good as they're going to feel all day.
Frank Sinatra, singer, who according to legend was buried with a flask of Jack Daniel's whiskey

DID YOU KNOW?

Bourbon gets its name from Bourbon County in Kentucky, where it was first made.

There were 2.5 billion litres-pure-alcohol of whisky stored in bonded warehouses in Scotland in 1994, worth about £20,000,000,000 at sale.

A single barrel of whisky contains about 500 litres of spirit; 1-2% of alcohol is lost each year through evaporation as it matures.

Cardow distillery is the only malt distillery started by a woman.

REAGAN'S BLUE BACKGROUND

When genealogists were looking into the family background of newly elected American President Ronald Reagan in the 1980s, they discovered that he was in fact a direct descendant of the great Blue family, one of the last of the great illegal Victorian whisky distilling and smuggling families.

The Blue family operated near Ballochroy, on the Kintyre peninsula in western Scotland. The whisky produced by the notorious Mary Blue was said to be far superior to many legitimate brands. She worked with her husband John McKinlay and her smuggler brother Johnny Blue (who died aged nearly 90 in 1895), and the gang was so successful that they even gave their different whiskies names – as if their business was all above board. Their two famous brands were Daylight (strong) and Moonlight (incredibly strong).

The Blue family's success was based largely on their skill as smugglers – they developed special casks that were fitted with a special compartment at both ends. If the barrel was opened at either end by the excisemen they merely found it was filled with butter or some other innocuous substance, but what they didn't realise was that four inches below the layer of butter was another wooden barrier beneath which lay several gallons of whisky.

WHISKY IS GO-GO

The notorious Whisky A Go-Go nightclub on Sunset Strip on Sunset Boulevard in Los Angeles has a celeb-soaked and somewhat debauched history.

Opening in January 1963, it is probably most famous as being the place where Jim Morrison and The Doors started out – they were the house band there in 1966. The Who, The Kinks, The Byrds, Led Zeppelin, AC/DC and Jimi Hendrix have also all played there, making it a world famous venue for music groupies.

It was also the epicentre of go-go dancing in America in the 1960s, causing uproar when dancers stripped entirely to their birthday suits suspended in cages in the club. On their first visit to LA, The Beatles also put in an appearance at the club after an invite from legendary screen blonde Jayne Mansfield.

The celebs stopped coming after the rise of punk though and the club fell on hard times in the early 1980s and closed its doors in 1982.

WHISKY MYTHS

WC Fields has to be one of the most famous Hollywood consumers of whisky in history, but most of the stories about him have been hugely exaggerated over the years.

In Fields' early days in the theatre after World War I, he was actually a juggler who spent days, weeks and months perfecting his act. No one who drank whisky at the rate claimed for Fields could have juggled at all, let alone have done it with the consummate skill he achieved. That said, there is no doubt that by the time his film career had really taken off, Fields was drinking a lot of whisky. But as one of his fellow actors recalled long after the great man's death: 'He was one of those rare people who can drink steadily all day and still appear to be completely sober.'

Fields was probably almost continually drunk on whisky, but at a low level – a level that created the character who is now remembered with such enormous affection. The classic WC Fields character – laconic, drawling, slow moving and ascerbically witty – was the real WC Fields and not a character developed for Hollywood. The character was created by Fields' love of whisky, but the legends of the huge quantities of whisky he put away are simply that – legends.

Fields was what today we might have called a functional alcoholic – he drank too much, but he knew what he was doing and it never got completely out of control.

MALT ART

Visitors to the famous whisky maker Glenfiddich can sample the company's products and then visit the gallery in the former distillery shop where the company has collected an astonishing array of art works ranging from paintings, photography, sculptures and mixed media to video and art installations.

The Glenfiddich Artists in Residence scheme has been described as a 'cocktail of malt whisky and visual art'. An annual budget of around £100,000 pays for a curator and for the services of eight artists in residence.

The artists live in former distillery workers' cottages and they can go wherever they like in the distillery from the warehouse to the bottling hall.

They can create whatever they like and install it wherever they choose, as long as they leave at least one piece at Glenfiddich when they leave.

The curator selects eight artists every year to stay at the distillery, and they often come from the most far flung corners of Europe. The hope is that all will find a unique inspiration at Glenfiddich, but it is difficult to know how much they are allowed to drink during their stay.

However, artists in the past have got along very well with the workforce – though some staff have admitted that they can't quite work out what some of the most outrageous artists are actually on about!

TWENTIETH-CENTURY WHISKY DRINKERS

Winston Churchill
Ernest Hemingway
Camilla Parker Bowles
Prince Charles
Franklin D Roosevelt
Dylan Thomas

UPSETTING

The Register of the Scottish Privy Council of 1614 includes a reference to distilling in a private house in the parish of Gamrie in Banffshire. The Register describes a burglary of a small house where the culprit is accused of breaking and entering, assault and upsetting a bottle of aqua vitae.

WHISKY THE FISH SAVER

Dr Edgar Stanhope, an Oxford scientist who was also a keen angler, carried out a number of experiments using whisky as a means of restoring life to dying fish. Having kept a trout out of water until it had apparently died, he would then drop it into a bucket filled with undiluted whisky. On the first occasion he tried this he commented: 'It was highly interesting to see the plucky manner a trout battled with his fainting condition after a dose of whisky, and came out the conqueror.'

On his next visit to the Wye river, Dr Stanhope took his bucket of whisky out in the boat – to the amusement of the local gillies – and tried the same experiment with a salmon. The results were less impressive, as Stanhope himself admitted: 'Strange to say, the salmon did not once attempt to rouse himself after being dosed, the consequence being fatal to him. This was the only fish that succumbed under the treatment.'

Bickerdyke then tried the experiment with a few coarse fish. He was most impressed by the effect of whisky on the dace. 'I had him out of the water three times of five minutes each. He was exceedingly faint and almost dead, but immediately the whisky was given he pulled himself together and in the course of a few minutes not only recovered, but darted around with a rapidity positively amazing.'

FRENCH TIPPLE

Few people would guess that the French – despite their love for wine and brandy – actually have more whisky distilleries than Ireland. That may not be saying much given how few there are in Ireland, but it is indicative of the value the French place on one of the world's great drinks.

The Distillerie Dikansky, based in Antrain in Brittany, near the Mont Saint-Michel – has been making Le Biniou (biniou means bagpipe) since about 1970. They import Scottish malt whisky and blend it with a locally distilled grain whisky. The Jacques Fisselier Company based in Rennes makes something called Glenroc – a pure grain whisky – as well as a blend known as Whisky de Bretagne.

Based near Reims, the Guillon distillery makes a single malt known as Guillon which involves drying the malt using the smoke from beech and oak leaves.

Other French whiskies include: Armorik, a single malt, Whisky Breton and Wambrechies.

THE CAMPBELLS ARE COMING...

According to the *Statistical Account of Scotland* for 1795,
whisky distilling in Campbeltown was as follows:

Location	No of stills	Bolls distilled	Produce in gallons
In the town	22	5,500	19,800
In the country	10	2,134	6,350
Total	32	7,634	26,150

DRAM-ATIC WRITING

Scotland, my auld, respected mither!
Tho' whiles ye moistify your leather,
Till, whare ye sit on craps o' heather,
Ye tine your dam;
Freedom an' whisky gang thegither!
Tak aff your dram!

Robbie Burns, *Tam O'Shanter*

NO WHISKY FAN

The Great War disrupted whisky production badly as supplies of barley to distilleries were severely restricted. David Lloyd George, the British Prime Minister at the time, was not sympathetic – largely because he was a temperance movement enthusiast and had no time at all for drinkers. In fact, so keen was he on teetotalism that Prohibition became a serious possibility.

George realised that the reaction against this would be massive, so he settled on a compromise. In 1915, the Immature Spirits Act was designed to reduce consumption by insisting that all whisky be allowed to mature for at least two years. In 1916 the rule was changed to three years. So, ironically, one of the factors that is now proudly proclaimed as signifying the quality of Scottish whisky was actually introduced in an attempt to stop us drinking the stuff. In 1917 the tax on whisky was doubled and a fixed price imposed. Whisky production was also banned completely. Later, Prohibition in America, followed by the Wall Street crash and world recession, meant that many of the distilleries that had tried to reopen when the war ended failed. That explains why a century and more ago there were so many more distilleries than there are today.

SAVED BY THE BELL

In Victorian times at some Scottish distilleries a curious – and somewhat benevolent – rule allowed workers to stop for a dram each time a bell rang.

It rang four times a day.

QUOTE UNQUOTE

The Scotch [sic] do not drink... During the whole of two or three pleasant weeks spent lecturing in Scotland, I never on any occasions saw whisky made use of as a beverage. I have seen people take it, of course, as a medicine, or as a precaution, or as a wise offset against a rather treacherous climate; but as a beverage, never.
Stephen Leacock, author and humorist

BOOZE IN THE BUDGET

There is a strange tradition in the Houses of Parliament that the Chancellor of the Exchequer is allowed to drink alcohol while delivering the Budget to the House. No other person is allowed to drink in the House of Commons chamber and there is no other occasion except for this, when alcohol is allowed in the House.

Despite this rare opportunity to have a tipple during proceedings, not all Chancellors have taken the opportunity. Gordon Brown has always opted for Scottish water.

John Major was also a water drinker during his time as Chancellor, while Jim Callaghan chose tonic water. Benjamin Disraeli also elected to stay in the sober camp by drinking milk during his Budgets.

However some have decided to take advantage of the alcohol opportunity. Winston Churchill, though known to enjoy whisky, drank brandy at Budget time and Geoffrey Howe sipped gin and tonics.

But some have made whisky their Budget drink of choice. Kenneth Clarke went for straight whisky while Nigel Lawson preferred to add a little water.

Some of the drink options were a little less appealing though; Derick Heathcote Amory, who was Chancellor between 1958 and 1960, drank milk, honey and rum, and Gladstone drank a mixture of sherry and egg – a combination one diarist of the time described as resembling a hair preparation.

Maybe he should have stuck to a single malt.

DRINKER, TAILOR, SOLDIER, SAILOR

The 10 professions that most enjoyed whisky in 1900 were:

Carpenters
Clergymen
Dancing masters
Dentists
Doctors
Journalists
Members of Parliament
Members of the House of Lords
Ship's captains
Train drivers

THE HARD STUFF

How is malt whisky made?
Answer on page 153.

DEATH'S FAVOURITE DRINK

Joseph Henry Blackburne (1841-1924) was a British chess player who picked up a rather menacing nickname – Black Death. He gained the nickname because of his large black beard and his extremely aggressive style of play. On one occasion his style left the chessboard and he threw an opponent who had just beaten him out of the window. Luckily for the contestant they were playing on the ground floor and he escaped with his life, if not his dignity.

Blackburne dominated the world of chess in the late nineteenth century and when he wasn't challenging for the British Championship he made a good living from exhibition matches, where he would often play blindfolded.

And what did Mr Blackburne attribute his success to? Well, whisky of course! He was not shy about his fondness for whisky and said that drinking it cleared his brain and improved his play. During one exhibition match at Cambridge University the students thought that exploiting Blackburne's propensity for whisky was their best chance of beating the champion. They placed a bottle at each end of the table to try and tempt him into drunkenness, a tactic they hoped would unravel his play. Unfortunately for them Blackburne was not so easily outdone and he reportedly drank both bottles and won every game in record time!

The attempt to ban alcohol in America – the Prohibition Era of 1920-1933 – was one of the greatest disasters of twentieth-century social policy. Alcohol may be bad for you, it may be the cause of motoring and other accidents – not to mention numerous social problems – but banning the world's oldest and most popular habits was never going to work. Once alcohol was outlawed, the pleasure-loving people of America simply got their supplies from illegal sources.

Alcohol supply became central to the huge fortunes amassed by criminals like Al Capone. But the curious thing is, that since alcohol was perfectly respectable in much of the rest of the world, American criminal gangs could buy it perfectly legitimately. Which is how one of London's most respectable and ancient wine merchants is said to have become involved in keeping America supplied with whisky during the 13 years of Prohibition. Berry Bros & Rudd has been supplying wine and spirits since the seventeenth century, so when an American walked into the shop and ordered several hundred cases of whisky, they probably thought nothing of it. But bootlegger Jack 'Legs' Diamond was planning to take his whisky where whisky drinking was no longer allowed.

It is ironic that during Prohibition demand for whisky in America increased. This meant a boost in business for many of Britain's whisky sellers – including Berry Bros.

There is evidence to suggest that big orders for whisky and other alcoholic drinks were delivered to Nassau in the Bahamas which was still then a British colony. Certainly Berry Bros shipped a great deal of Cutty Sark Whisky into the Bahamas at this time and – according to legend – that whisky was then taken out into international waters off the New Jersey coast where it was sold on to American gangsters.

Scottish distillers did a roaring trade, as did the London-based merchants and since they were shipping to a British colony it was all perfectly legal. Those who think it's all a myth need only look at the figures: in 1918, before Prohibition, the citizens of the Bahamas were knocking back some 944 gallons of whisky a year; by 1922 they were apparently drinking more than 386,000 gallons a year! Sales of whisky to other British islands near the US mainland also increased substantially – islands like the Turks and Caycos Islands, and Grand Cayman.

The American government complained to the British government about the exports of whisky to their colonies, but nothing was done. The trade as far as the islands was legal and one suspects that the British government knew that the American law against alcohol was ultimately unenforceable.

Medieval dinners without whisky were clearly a bore!

QUOTE UNQUOTE

*A woman drove me to drink and I didn't even
have the decency to thank her.*
WC Fields, comedian and whisky aficionado

HALLUCI-NATION

When whisky was first invented, it must have seemed the most extraordinary stuff. With no knowledge of intoxicants, early drinkers no doubt felt that the wonderful feelings whisky induced were due to supernatural powers – which may explain the fact that the Celts called it the 'water of life'. Even today in remote parts of the world, beliefs not dissimilar to those still hold sway. Among the Yamamami of the Amazon, an intoxicating drink made from water and fermented grain is still very popular, but it is drunk largely to induce hallucinations – the kind that only really heavy drinkers in the West still experience. The Yamamami drink copious quantities of their 'whisky' and then produce carvings, paintings, music and dancing – without their 'whisky' they are apparently unable to do anything creative at all!

MORE SCOTTISH THAN THE SCOTTISH?

In Japan the Yoichi whisky distillery produces a rich, peaty malt that is said to get its flavour from what is known as direct heating distillation. For this, pot stills are heated with coal, the traditional method that has vanished almost entirely even from Scotland.

INGREDIENTS FOR SUCCESS

Rob Roy

A dram of Scotch
A dash of sweet Vermouth
A dash of Angostura bitters

Scotch Fizz

A dram of Scotch
Fraise chilled champagne
A strawberry

THE WHISKY SHIP

The ghostly tale of the Phantom Whisky Ship of Chaleur Bay in North America is a tale of treachery and deception. It centres on a Portuguese explorer called Gaspar Cort-Real and his brother Miguel, who landed at Chaleur Bay, probably in 1500.

Gaspar traded whisky and some guns to the native Americans in return for furs. But on one occasion he also enticed a group of Indians aboard the ship, gave them enough whisky to drink themselves into a stupor and then chained them up to be taken to Portugal and sold as slaves.

He made money, became greedy and thought he could repeat the trick, but the Indians had not forgotten, nor forgiven. They boarded the Portuguese trader's ship as it lay at anchor and killed everyone except Gaspar himself. They chained him to a rock and watched as the tide rose and he drowned – they also took his huge cargo of whisky and then left his ship floating empty and at anchor in the bay.

Two years later Gaspar's brother Miguel came in search of him. With his men they boarded the ship but were immediately attacked by the Indians who had learned by now never to trust Europeans. Rather than be killed by the Indians, Miguel and his men set fire to the ship and drank whisky as the flames licked up around them. None survived but every now and then – the last sighting was in the late 1990s – the ghostly whisky ship is seen far out in the bay and still in flames.

CLASSIC RECIPES

Atholl Brose
Mix equal amounts of honey and oatmeal in a small amount of cold water. Add a dram or two of whisky and stir till frothy. Keep in a sealed bottle for a few days, then drink. Two pints of whisky are needed for half a pound of honey and half a pound of oatmeal.

Whisky Mac
Mix whisky and Crabbies green ginger wine in proportions that suit you best.

Whisky Sour
Pour a large whisky; add the juice from half a lemon and half a teaspoonful of sugar. Add plenty of ice, shake vigorously and serve with soda water.

QUOTE UNQUOTE

There is no such thing as bad whiskey. Some whiskeys just happen to be better than others. But a man shouldn't fool with booze until he's 50; then he's a damn fool if he doesn't.
William Faulkner, novelist

ANGER MANAGEMENT

In his Highland Sports, *published in 1885, salmon-fishing and whisky-drinking fanatic Alexander MacGregor recalled the remarkable power of the amber nectar to bring people together.*

An angler on a stretch of water was fishing quite happily when a giant of a man approached him in full Highland dress angrily brandishing a large wooden club. Before the by now terrified angler lay the water, too deep to wade; behind him approached the ferocious foe. The unoffending fisherman expected to be hurled into the water by his fierce assailant, whose anger knew no bounds when he was informed by the fisherman that he, the fisherman, understood the visitor at the Dunalastair Hotel had the right of angling in the river. The poor fisherman took the wisest course and apologised profusely before producing a wellfilled flask. He lubricated his apologies with neat whisky.

Within half an hour, such is the power of the single malt, the two men had become the greatest of friends. And then it was that the Highlander, upon learning the name of his unconscious offender, granted to him and his progeny until the third or fourth generation the right of fishing the water whenever and wherever they chose.

WRIST ACTION

Most hospitals in England, Wales and Scotland are busiest on Friday and Saturday evenings because that's when people between 18 and 25 go out, get drunk and either fall over or beat each other up.

The binge-drinking phenomena has baffled social scientists and politicians for the past decade and various theories have been put forward to explain the peculiarly British attitude to alcohol. The generally accepted explanation is that the British are addicted to the idea of celebration – when the week's work has finished they head off to pubs and clubs to get outrageously drunk because a huge celebration matches their mood of elation.

Politicians and other more sober-minded elders who put their heads together to try to get to grips with the social costs of drunkenness approached a group of scientists. Was there anything they could do to help? An American scientist then remembered an elderly friend of his who had long enjoyed whisky to the exclusion of all other drinks, but who had so worried about over indulging in his favourite tipple that he had created a device to tell him when he was in danger of going too far.

Invented in 1992, the drinking bracelet contains a simple counting mechanism and an alarm. The old whisky drinker used to set it to allow himself five small glasses – if he exceeded this number the bracelet would let out a high-pitched electronic squawk. But how did it know when he'd exceeded his limit? Easy – the bracelet registered a drink every time he lifted his hand to his mouth. That initially raised the slight difficulty that the inventor had to calculate in advance how many sips it would take to finish his dram, but once he'd made the calculation the bracelet made him stick to the deal he'd made with it when sober.

BABY SOOTHER

A train crash on the outskirts of Birmingham in the 1880s proved advantageous for residents of what was then one of the poorest parts of Britain. The reason? The train was loaded with thousands of bottles of whisky from a number of distilleries. What shocked the police was not the fact that the local residents had managed to spirit away every last bottle within minutes of the crash happening; nor was it that little was done to help the injured driver. What really shocked the police was that the whisky was soon being sold in small bottles on the streets as a means to keep babies from crying!

ODDBALL MIXERS

Among the oddest things whisky has been mixed with:

Cucumber
Double cream
Fresh strawberries
Grapes
Horseradish
Lemon
Lime
Melted chocolate
Orange juice

CELLULOID WHISKY

Whisky has been central to Hollywood for almost a century – where would the classic cowboy film be, for example, without those fearsome looming whisky shots thrown back in a thousand dusty Wild West bars?

Whisky means style, toughness, rebellion and ultra cool, and whisky was itself one of the first products to realise the advertising power of film – Dewar's Scotch organised an advertising film for its own products at the very dawn of cinema history in 1897. According to one commentator, the film shows 'bemused actors dressed in kilts performing a very poor impression of a Highland fling.'

From here on in every cowboy and gangster film for the next century and more showed whisky as the tough-guy drink – at least that is until the 2003 film *Lost in Translation*, which taps into the Japanese love of whisky, but shows a bemused and frankly bored American actor (played by Bill Murray) trying to film an ad for Suntory Whisky. For Bill Murray the image of sophistication the Japanese are trying to portray through the ad is bunkum – but for the Japanese, whisky is still the tough, cool drink that it always was in American film.

The Japanese – and for that matter the Chinese – use whisky throughout their film industry to indicate status, which is hardly surprising given that they have taken to whisky the way the Americans took to it at the turn of the nineteenth century. It's drunk when friends meet, its drunk before dinner, after dinner, at parties and weddings, in bars and clubs – and it is drunk in very large quantities indeed. China, for example, consumes a staggering 10 billion cases of spirits annually, much of it, whisky.

IT'S THE WHISKY TALKING

'I wish I didn't have to drink this damned sherry!'

THE HARD STUFF

What was meant by proof spirit?
Answer on page 153.

A LETTER FROM THE POET

Sir,

Allow us, Sir, yet farther, just to hint at another rich vein of comfort in the dreary regions of Adversity; the gratulations of an approving conscience. In a certain great Assembly of which you are a distinguished member, panegyrics on your private virtues have so often wounded your delicacy, that we shall not distress you with any thing on the subject. There is, however, one part of your public conduct which our feelings will not permit us to pass in silence – our gratitude must trespass on your modesty – we mean, worthy Sir, the whole of your behaviour to the Scots Distillers. In evil hours, when obtrusive memory presses bitterly on the sense, let that recollection come, Sir, like a healing angel, and speak the peace to your soul which the world can neither give nor take away.

We have the honour to be, Sir
Your grateful, sympathising, humble servants

John Barleycorn

From Robbie Burns' open letter to William Pitt the Younger, published in the *Edinburgh Evening Courant* of 9 February 1789

Ships, tanks and aeroplanes designed for war can always be improved, but what looks good on the drawing board doesn't always work in the real world – as the whisky-loving Russian Admiral Popov discovered in 1873. That was the year that saw the launch of one of the strangest military machines ever invented.

It was early one autumn morning that the warship *Novgorod* put to sea from the Black Sea port of Nikolaiev. Rumour had been rife for months among the inhabitants of the town that this was to be no ordinary launch and as the ship hit the water, there were gasps of astonishment. At more than 2,500 tonnes the *Novgorod* was big for her time; she was also bristling with armaments – and perfectly circular.

Popov had been faced with a difficult design problem – he needed a warship that could operate in shallow coastal waters, but he had been given a lengthy list of armaments by the Czar and was told that everything on the list had to be on the ship. The Czar – who was paranoid that his country was in danger of invasion – had put so many things on the list that a conventional warship small enough to do the work of patrolling inlets and bays would have sunk under the weight of armaments. The *Novgorod* was the solution, but rumour has it that Popov – whose great love in life was whisky – had designed it after enjoying a whole bottle of his favourite imported spirit.

Be that as it may, the new warship had a shallow draught and being circular could achieve angles of fire from its myriad weapons that were only dreamt of on conventional warships – in theory it was a remarkably innovative craft. But what was it like in practice?

The *Novgorod* had a central tower fitted with two massive 10-tonne guns that could be turned full circle; the ship was kitted out with no less than 12 powerful screw propellers and, properly used, they could propel the ship forward or backward or even make it spin rapidly clockwise or anticlockwise. The sailors who manned the *Novgorod* reported that it was unusually stable even in rough weather.

The biggest drawback to the circular warship and the main reason only two were ever built was that they were very slow. With a top speed of about 10 knots they could never compete in open water with more conventional ships, and with no keel and a very shallow draught they were incredibly difficult to steer at all – one captain reported that steering the *Novgorod* was like ice-skating with butter on the soles of your boots! Another Captain said: 'Only a drunk could have designed a warship like this!'

At three o'clock on the afternoon there was a loud peal at the bell, an authoritative voice in the hall, and, to my surprise, no less a person than Mr. Athelney Jones was shown up to me. Very different was he, however, from the brusque and masterful professor of common sense who had taken over the case so confidently at Upper Norwood. His expression was downcast, and his bearing meek and even apologetic.

'Good-day, sir; good-day,' said he. 'Mr. Sherlock Holmes is out, I understand.'

'Yes, and I cannot be sure when he will be back. But perhaps you would care to wait. Take that chair and try one of these cigars.'

'Thank you; I don't mind if I do,' said he, mopping his face with a red bandanna handkerchief.

'And a whisky and soda?'

'Well, half a glass. It is very hot for the time of year, and I have had a good deal to worry and try me.

Arthur Conan Doyle, *The Sign of Four*

ONE FOR THE KIRK

Life is always difficult for the churchman who likes to drink. In the Anglican and Catholic churches drinking in moderation is just about tolerated, but among the stricter protestant sects, particularly the Presbyterians, the very idea of drink is anathema. Which creates the curious paradox that the country that produces some of the most delicious alcoholic drink in the world – namely Scotland – also produces some of the strictest Presbyterians. Occasionally drink and Presbyterianism do battle and drink is invariably the winner.

A classic case occurred when the stationmaster at Mallaig spoke to the purser of the West Highland steamer which had just berthed after a journey from the Isle of Lewis in the Outer Hebrides – an island famous for putting padlocks on the children's swings to prevent fun on the Sabbath.

The stationmaster shouted to the purser: 'Any goods for the Glasgow train?' 'Aye,' came the answer. 'Two jars of whisky.'

But having been told to expect whisky, the stationmaster was astonished to see a large flour barrel and an earthenware jar swung aboard. 'But that's not a whisky jar!' he shouted.

'Oh don't worry yersel,' came the reply. 'The jar is for the established church minister. The other – the flour barrel – has a whisky jar hidden in it for the Free Kirk minister!'

WIT AND WHISKY

A professor of chemistry wanted to teach his fifth-grade class a lesson about the evils of liquor, so he produced an experiment that involved a glass of water, a glass of whisky and two worms.

'Now, class. Observe closely the worms,' he said, putting a worm first into the water. The worm in the water writhed about, happy as a worm in water could be. The second worm, he put into the whisky. It writhed painfully, and quickly sank to the bottom, dead as a doornail. 'Now, what lesson can we derive from this experiment?' the professor asked.

Little Johnny, sitting in the back, raised his hand and replied: 'Drink whisky and you won't get worms.'

QUOTE UNQUOTE

Whisky makes me sorry
Whisky makes me glad
Whisky makes me love the world
Whisky makes me mad
Traditional song

IT ALL BEGAN IN 1066

Glenmorangie Distillery is located in The Royal Burgh of Tain, the oldest burgh in Scotland.

In 1066, King Malcolm III of Scotland granted Tain the right of 'immunity' creating an area of sanctuary within the town's limits. Important tax exemptions were also extended to the merchants of Tain. However, at the start of 1066, Edward the Confessor, Ruler of England for 23 years, died without leaving an heir to the throne. This historic event was to change the country for ever as a fight for the crown began in earnest.

By the end of the year, a Norman called William the Conqueror would be king. He defeated Edward's successor, Harold, at one of the most famous battles on English soil: the Battle of Hastings, immortalised today in the Bayeaux Tapestry.

During the battle, Margaret, the niece of Edward the Confessor, sought refuge from the Norman invaders in the court of King Malcolm III. Malcolm and Margaret married that year, making her queen of Scotland.

WHISKY AFICIONADOS

Whisky lover	Most-loved whisky
Nicolas Cage	Macallan
Sven-Goran Eriksson	Glenmorangie
Ernest Hemingway	Johnnie Walker, Red Label
Princess Margaret	Famous Grouse
Tom Selleck	Glenmorangie
Queen Victoria	Royal Lochnagar

FULL OF FLAVOUR

**Whisky descriptions that suggest that the liquid in
your glass just might be something else**

Appley • Biscuity
Custardy • Doggy
Floral • Fruity
Grassy • Honey
Nutty • Peaty
Sexy • Yeasty
Bloody awful!

DRAM-ATIC WRITING

She had, none the less, to give her mind steadily to what Mr. Mudge had again written her about, the idea of her applying for a transfer to an office quite similar – she couldn't yet hope for a place in a bigger – under the very roof where he was foreman, so that, dangled before her every minute of the day, he should see her, as he called it, "hourly," and in a part, the far N.W. district, where, with her mother, she would save on their two rooms alone nearly three shillings. It would be far from dazzling to exchange Mayfair for Chalk Farm, and it wore upon her much that he could never drop a subject; still, it didn't wear as things HAD worn, the worries of the early times of their great misery, her own, her mother's and her elder sister's – the last of whom had succumbed to all but absolute want when, as conscious and incredulous ladies, suddenly bereft, betrayed, overwhelmed, they had slipped faster and faster down the steep slope at the bottom of which she alone had rebounded. Her mother had never rebounded any more at the bottom than on the way; had only rumbled and grumbled down and down, making, in respect of caps, topics and "habits", no effort whatever – which simply meant smelling much of the time of whiskey.

Henry James, *In the Cage*

END OF AN ERA

When Sir James Matheson bought the Isle of Lewis in Scotland's Outer Hebrides in 1844, it meant the end of a long tradition of whisky-making because Sir James Matheson was a rabid abstainer and prohibitionist. He had the local distillery demolished and built Lews Castle, a mock-Tudor edifice on the site.

QUOTE UNQUOTE

Champagne's funny stuff. I'm used to whiskey. Whiskey is a slap on the back, and champagne's a heavy mist before my eyes.
Jimmy Stewart, actor

WHISKY EATS

Lamb Chops with Fresh Figs and Whisky

4-6 baby lamb chops, $1\frac{1}{2}$ tbsp olive oil, 1tsp butter, 1tbsp shallot (chopped), 1 clove garlic (chopped), $1\frac{1}{2}$ tsp coarsely ground black pepper, $\frac{1}{2}$ tsp red peppercorns, $1\frac{1}{4}$ quart cups very rich veal stock, $\frac{1}{4}$ cup single malt, 4 fresh figs (carefully peeled and quartered at room temperature), 4 rosemary stalks, $\frac{1}{2}$ cup dried cherries (soaked in 6tbsp of slightly warmed whisky for 1 hour), $\frac{1}{3}$ cup medium Scotch barley, $1\frac{1}{2}$ cups water.

1. Bring $1\frac{1}{2}$ cups of water to the boil, add barley and $\frac{1}{2}$ cup veal stock, cover and simmer for 45 minutes or until all liquid is absorbed.

2. Stir in soaked cherries and peppercorns and cover. (Save 15 cherries for the lamb dish.)

3. Sauté shallot and garlic in oil and butter over low heat. When soft, remove half. Raise heat to medium, add lamb chops and cook for 3 minutes on each side.

4. Lower heat, add $\frac{3}{4}$ cup veal stock, black pepper and whisky.

5. Remove chops and cover, simmer sauce, add salt to taste, add 15 dried cherries and reduce sauce by about a third.

6. Season barley and place on plates; arrange chops and figs on barley bed, spoon sauce over and garnish with rosemary stalks.

CARRY AS CARRY CAN

Before glass bottles and in the days of illegal distilling, whisky was
regularly carried across the hills in wooden barrels but also in:

Hollowed out logs
Leather buckets
Pig's bladders
Sheep's gut
Stone jars

MAN-SIZED WHISKY

The last native speaker of Manx
– the Gaelic spoken on the Isle of
Man, off the north-west coast of
England – died in the 1970s.
Manx was lucky to have lasted
so long, simply because of the
small size of the island, and the
decline of the language seems to
have mirrored the decline of
whiskey-making on the island.

Distilling was certainly a feature
of island life in the eighteenth
century. Isolated in the Irish Sea
midway between England and
Ireland it was the perfect staging
post for smugglers, but also
produced its own fine whiskey.

The Revestment Act of 1767
imposed severe penalties on
distillers – £200 plus the forfeiture
of produce and equipment – but
by the early 1800s, distilling was
still taking place. The hereditary
owner of the island, the Duke of
Atholl, complained to the
Treasury that the common people
were enjoying themselves too
much on liquor for which they
were not paying tax. An 1826 Act
of Parliament and another of
1867 increased the penalties for

distilling and there were no legal
distilleries on the island, but it is
unlikely that all the illegal stills
were closed on an island so far
from mainland Britain.

In 1976 it at last became a legal
possibility to start making
whiskey again on the island
when the 1867 Act was repealed.
A distillery was set up at Kella
Mills and a white spirit known
as Manx Whiskey began to be
produced. This was a blend
based on whisky imported from
Scotland and then redistilled.
Then in the 1990s the Glen Kella
Distillery was taken to court by
some of the world's biggest
distillery owners to stop them
calling their product whiskey.

Glen Kella lost the case and
changed the name of their
whiskey to Manx Spirit, but it
was all nonsense, given that the
three-year maturation rule –
which the big distilleries had used
to close Glen Kella – was an
arbitrary rule anyway and
imposed early in the twentieth
century to reduce the amount of
whisky coming on to the market.

TWO RULES

There are two rules when drinking whisky:
1. Never drink whisky without adding water;
2. Never drink water without adding whisky.

COCKTAILS THAT INCLUDE WHISKY
AS THE MAIN INGREDIENT

Alabama Slammer Shooter
Alaskan Pipeline • Amenie Mama
Anaconda Shot • Apple Jack
Banana Jack • Bart Simpson
Bee Stinger (Wildman Style)
Bend Me Over Slammer
Be Sweet • Black Allocation
Black Dragon • Black Jack WV
Black Tooth • Blood of Satan
Blue Blazer • Blue Caboose • Blue Flush
Boomerang Shot • Boot to the Head
Buffalo Sweat • Burning Cherry
Burnt Turkey

DRAM-ATIC WRITING

As to daily news, there is no dearth of that commodity. This passenger is reported to have lost fourteen pounds at Vingt-et-un in the saloon yesterday; and that passenger drinks his bottle of champagne every day, and how he does it (being only a clerk), nobody knows. The head engineer has distinctly said that there never was such times – meaning weather – and four good hands are ill, and have given in, dead beat. Several berths are full of water, and all the cabins are leaky. The ship's cook, secretly swigging damaged whiskey, has been found drunk; and has been played upon by the fire-engine until quite sober. All the stewards have fallen down-stairs at various dinner-times, and go about with plasters in various places. The baker is ill, and so is the pastry-cook. A new man, horribly indisposed, has been required to fill the place of the latter officer; and has been propped and jammed up with empty casks in a little house upon deck, and commanded to roll out pie-crust, which he protests (being highly bilious) it is death to him to look at. News! A dozen murders on shore would lack the interest of these slight incidents at sea.

Charles Dickens, *American Notes*

GOING, GOING, GONE

In a sale of ephemera at a London auction house at the turn of the century, the following items were sold:

Two 1940s whisky bottle labels

An eighteenth-century whisky bottle (empty)

A Victorian whisky bottle label

Five empty Victorian whisky bottles

Two early twentieth-century sample bottles

Two whisky poster advertisements form the 1930s

THE HARD STUFF

How soon after it is distilled is whisky usually sold?
Answer on page 153.

NO WHISKY FOR THE JUNIORS

During the Great War, the curious traditions of the officers' mess were by and large intended to stay there. Some, as is the way with these things, leaked out however. For example, new officers were treated appallingly badly as part of a bizarre initiation period and as the drinking of whisky was central to mess traditions (and an almost continuous pleasure in the evenings) – new officers weren't allowed to drink whisky at all.

Older officers made a point of enjoying their whisky and while they were at it treated the juniors with open contempt. Whisky was always served in the mess almost from the moment the officers sat down to dinner and to add to the humiliation, the waiters were told to offer it to young recruits. But if they showed any interest or indicated they would like some the waiters were to tell them it was not allowed.

This bizarre whisky ritual – just one of many similar petty rituals designed purely to humiliate new recruits – led to one young officer arriving early at the mess and urinating in the bottles of whisky that had been left to breathe before the officers arrived. Ironically, what he didn't realise was that as he had now been attending the officers' mess for several weeks, he was entitled at last to drink whisky himself. When the waiter approached him, he expected the usual rebuff but was actually offered a large tumbler full!

Now he found himself in a tricky position – not to drink whisky when offered would have been a dreadful faux pas, so the poor young man was obliged to swallow the whole glass in one mouthful!

INGREDIENTS FOR SUCCESS

Highland Fling

A dram of Scotch
A dash of sweet Vermouth
2 dashes of orange bitters
An olive

WHISKY AND OYSTERS

If you happen to be travelling through the vast, dry, open spaces of mid America and you suddenly feel hungry, most of what you'll find on the menu of pretty much every restaurant you might encounter will be pretty predictable: vast steaks, eggs, burgers and fries – in short, all the usual things one associates with cattle-rich America.

But many restaurants, particularly in small town Wyoming and Colorado, also offer what is known as Colorado (or Wyoming) oysters.

Now these States are a long way from the sea, which might make the naturally suspicious think twice before ordering. On the other hand, globalisation will make an equal number of us think how progressive America is that oysters can be flown to these dry inland towns just for the culinary pleasure of it.

If you order these American oysters you'll be surprised to see they look like they have been deep fried in batter and that they taste remarkably like chewy chicken. The reason is that they are actually bulls' testicles. Rather than waste the millions of testicles produced each year by the vast cattle industry, mid-western states long ago decided to utilise as much as they could of each animal.

In fact, recipes for testicles date back to the early days when settlers moved west and food was often in short supply. Like so many poor people around the world those frontiersmen made use of whatever they had, which is why when an animal was killed its fur or skin was used to make clothes or leather goods, and every part of the body was eaten.

The Great Depression of the 1920s and 1930s produced another surge of interest in eating testicles and what began as necessity became tradition which is why those restaurants so often include a few heritage dishes on their menus – bulls' testicles are best eaten, we are told by those who really know about these things, with several large shots of whisky.

Scotland, having eclipsed Ireland as the world's great centre of whisky production early in the twentieth century, is now the centre of world production. The country has a large number of modern, well-equipped distilleries which emphasise the traditional aspects of their craft, and finding a genuine traditional distillery is very difficult indeed.

But one old distillery that still gives at least an echo of how it used to be done is Bowmore. Situated on the shores of Loch Indaal, on the island of Islay in western Scotland, Bowmore started life as long ago as 1779. Whisky is produced here as it has always been produced and in all that time the distillery has been run by only five different owners – each inherited the traditions of his predecessor and did little to change them. The theory being that once you've discovered a system that produces fine whisky every time, don't change it – or change it at your peril. But in what sense is Bowmore traditional? Well, apart from the fact that Bowmore's equipment is pretty much as it has always been, the distillery also employs a maltman, a job that has long vanished from most distilleries.

The maltman turns the barley by hand on the malting floor using a wooden shovel. This is to ensure that the barley germinates perfectly and evenly before it enters the next stage of the manufacturing process. Bowmore whisky sells at a premium because it doesn't produce vast amounts and it has a unique position with access to rich peaty freshwater and air that blows in with a salty tang from the sea.

Bowmore's water comes from the nearby Laggan River. It would have fallen as rain some two thousand years ago and to reach the river it had to percolate slowly through rock and stone; the slowness of its journey allowed time for the water to absorb a unique mixture of minerals, a mixture that no other process can imitate. This slow maturation of water cannot be produced elsewhere, because the conditions that exist at Bowmore do not exist in precisely the same form anywhere else in the world. Unique water and sea breezes give Bowmore whisky a unique reputation among fans of the amber nectar.

But perhaps the most extraordinary thing about two hundred-plus-year-old Bowmore distillery is the vaults that lie beneath the main buildings. In other parts of the distillery there have been superficial changes over the centuries, as items have been repaired or replaced, but in the vaults all is as it was at the end of the eighteenth century.

Wherever you look in the damp gloomy vaults the spaces are filled with vast oak barrels where the whisky lies undisturbed, its unique blend of chemicals mingling and developing for years – decades even – before it is ready at last to be drunk.

IT'S THE WHISKY TALKING

Preparing a hot toddy – there's no scientific reason why hot whisky, water, honey and lemon juice should make you feel better, but it does!

QUOTE UNQUOTE

Truth implies more than a simple statement of fact. 'I don't have any whiskey' may be a fact, but it is not a truth.
William S Burroughs, writer

HOBBLE-DE-HOY

Mounted customs men in the nineteenth century were known as Hobblers. The reason: they rode Shetland ponies, their feet almost dragging on the ground, the pony appearing continually to stumble, or hobble along.

Londoner Alfred Barnard spent more than two years travelling Britain and Ireland by train, ship and horse and cart to visit every whisky distillery in England, Scotland and Ireland.

His book *The Whisky Distilleries of the United Kingdom* was published in 1887. Among the most interesting parts of his book is the list of Irish distilleries, almost all of which have now vanished:

Abbey Street, Londonderry
Avoniel, Belfast
Bandon, Bandon
Birr, Birr
Bishop's Water, Wexford
Bow Street, Dublin
Brusna, Kilbeggan
Bushmills, Bushmills
Coleraine, Coleraine
Dundalk, Dundalk
Glen, Kilnap
John's Lane, Dublin
Jones Road, Dublin
Limavady, Limavady
Limerick, Limerick
Marrowbone Lane, Dublin
Midleton, Midleton
Monasterevan, Monasterevan
North Mall, Cork
Nun's Island, Galway
Phoenix Park, Dublin
Royal Irish Distilleries, Belfast
The Irish Distillery, Belfast
The Lower Distillery, Comber
The Upper Distillery, Comber
Thomas Street, Dublin
Tullamore, Tullamore
Waterside, Londonderry

A LOAD OF OLD BOLLS

In 1494, the Scottish Exchequer Rolls provide us with the very first written reference to whisky; on the ancient cracking parchment can be read, by those still sober, the words: 'Eight bolls of malt sent this day to Friar John Cor wherewith to make aquavitae'.

74 *Number of empty whisky bottles used in an art student's 'installation' in 1976*

A HOT TODDY IN JUST A JIFFY

Three spoons of sugar dissolved with boiling water and lemon juice. Add Scotch and stir; pour in more boiling water and top up with whisky.

THE HARD STUFF

Is whisky made in Wales?
Answer on page 153.

MEDICINE MEN

Until the late nineteenth century, Scottish society was far more heavily influenced by alcohol than other parts of the UK. The writer JW Robertson Scott remembered that in the 1870s, when he was a child, anyone who called at the house would automatically be given claret or whisky – never tea or coffee. And every business meeting, however early in the morning, was conducted around a few glasses of whisky or wine.

The practice was based not entirely on simple hospitality but also on the ancient belief that alcohol was a cure-all – the fact that whisky was called the 'water of life' was, in other words, no coincidence. For centuries after whisky was first distilled and when medical knowledge was almost non-existent, whisky was given by physicians to their patients almost regardless of their symptoms.

There is evidence, too, that in the early days of whisky-making the task was given to particular families and those families tended to be traditionally associated with medicine.

Hereditary professions were an essential part of the clan-based way of life and members of the Clan MacBeatha (including variants like MacBethadh, MacBeth and Beaton) were Scotland's hereditary physicians. Their herbal cures may well have worked for a variety of ailments, but when they began to distil whisky and administer it, the effects were so immediate in comparison to herbal cures that it is no wonder their skill became legendary!

Members of that MacBeatha clan amassed a vast store of knowledge over the centuries, much of it from distant Arabic and Greek sources. Scotland's long love affair with medicine continues to this day, with an unusually high proportion of young Scots studying medicine. This can perhaps be traced back to this great hereditary tradition.

INGREDIENTS FOR SUCCESS

Purple Heather

A dram of Scotch
A tsp of Cassis
Ice

Mix together in a tall glass and add soda.

WEARY OF WHISKY?

Whisky is not the only Scottish fare you can enjoy; if you've had enough of whisky (as if!) then you could always cast your taste buds towards other Scottish food and drink.

Irn-Bru – The brightly coloured soft drink was originally marketed with the slogan: 'Made in Scotland from girders'. Apparently this did not stop it becoming the most popular soft drink in Scotland. Many people in fact use Irn-Bru as a mixer with alcoholic drinks, particularly vodka and whisky. It is also reputed to be an excellent hangover cure – so it might come in handy after a long night on the whisky.

Haggis – The granddaddy of all Scottish foods, haggis sounds a lot worse than it tastes. You take a sheep's heart, liver and lungs, and once they are minced together, you mix them with onion, oatmeal, suet, spices, salt and stock. The concoction is traditionally boiled in the animal's stomach for several hours. But don't worry if it doesn't sound too appealing, most recipes also recommend a large dose of whisky to be mixed in with the meat.

Cranachan – This traditional Scottish dessert is made by mixing whipped cream, whisky, honey and fresh raspberries together and topping it with toasted oatmeal. It's funny how whisky seems to keep popping up...

Deep-fried Mars Bar – No one knows exactly how this originated, but it seems that from the mid 1990s they were sold from chip shops around Scotland. Media interest/incredulity probably helped lengthen the fad and they seem set to stay, even if only for the benefit of tourists. The basic concept is simple: you put a Mars Bar in a deep fat fryer along with everything else that is being fried, which may include fish, chips and sausages. And as most chip shops in Scotland use beef dripping to fry with, a deep-fried Mars Bar can sometimes have a slightly beefy taste. Actually, maybe it would be safer to stick to the whisky after all.

DRAM-ATIC WRITING

'Fire on, fire on,' says Captain Ward, 'I value you not a pin;
If you are brass on the outside, I am steel within.
'Go home, go home,' says Captain Ward, 'And tell your King
from me,
If he reigns King upon dry land
I will reign at sea.'

Captain Ward and the Rainbow **song** lyrics

SOUND THE PART

**Sound like a whisky buff; take a sip, suck through your teeth, then
reel off any three of the following adjectives in slow succession.**

Amber
Challenging
Chocolate
Dour
Musty
Oily
Rugged
Smoky
Thrusting

WHISKY MYTHS

Before medicine became a genuinely scientific affair, all kinds of bizarre
concoctions were given to the sick in the hope that they would have
some effect: dried rats' urine and pounded seaweed was once
considered excellent for gallstones, for example. Whisky was once
central to medicine despite the fact that there was no hard evidence that
it was any good. Of course the initial euphoria created by drinking
whisky – in the days when the scientific effects of alcohol were not
understood – must have made it seem almost magical in properties.

In the Highlands it was given to fractious children; old people swore by
it (or swore after drinking it!) for rheumatism; any swellings or bruising
might be given a whisky poultice and for blocked ears whisky was once
though to be a tonic.

All of course are myths – whisky has few if any medicinal benefits other
than ultimately inducing unconsciousness – which must have been a
great relief to those facing surgery in the days before anaesthetics!

Firewater – as the native Americans called whisky – clearly brought life to tired limbs.

QUOTE UNQUOTE

Whiskey and beer are a man's worst enemies... but the man that runs away from his enemies is a coward!
Zeca Pagodinho, Brazilian songwriter

LUCKY 13

Whisky matures best in a damp environment and whisky manufacturers strive for the best conditions for their casks to wait out their decade or so of maturing. Even a small variation in humidity can change the flavour of a maturing whisky. Glenmorangie have noticed just that and have designated whisky that is stored in its cellar number 13 for a special expression.

What's so special about Cellar 13? Well, it's much closer to the Dornoch Firth, which leads into the North Sea, and so is cool and moist. This, and only using first fill casks gives Glenmorangie Cellar 13 a distinctive taste and has warranted the special bottling. Lucky for some.

Whisky-making started in the remote places of Scotland where outsiders rarely came. We know much about it from a traveller called Fynes Moryson, who published his *Itinerary* in 1617. It is a fascinating account, among other things, of the pleasures and pains of the English, Irish and the inhabitants of other nations. We know that Moryson visited Ireland and Scotland and he comments on the role of whisky. The Irish, he tells us, drink 'aqua-vitae, vulgarly called Usquebagh, the best in the world of that kind... and in many families (especially at feasts) both men and women use excess'.

Moryson also reveals just how different whisky production was at this time compared to today's. The natural conservatism of whisky drinkers clearly did not exist more than three and a half centuries ago and the inhabitants of the Highlands and Islands (and Ireland) were more than happy to experiment a little. The whisky of the Hebrides, Moryson tells us, came in a surprising number of varieties: pride of place seems to have gone to Usquebaugh which was a spirit twice distilled, like modern Scottish whisky. Then there is Trestarig – a three times distilled spirit (like modern Irish whiskey), and most intriguing of all, they drank something called Usquebaugh-baul, which was spirit distilled no less than four times. We don't really have any idea what these spirits tasted like, but they reveal that the rules that now strictly define Scottish whisky simply did not exist in earlier times.

Other travellers spoke highly (sometimes disparagingly) of the Celtic love of spirits, and in his description of the Western Islands of Scotland published in 1703 (in Gaelic as *Na h-Eileanan bho chionn trì cheud bliadhna*), Martin Martin tells us that on the island of Lewis in the Hebrides, spirits were so strong they were consumed in the smallest amounts:

'Their plenty of corn was such, as disposed the natives to brew several sorts of liquors, as common usquebaugh, another called trestarig, id est, aquavitæ, three times distilled, which is strong and hot; a third sort is four times distilled, and this by the natives is called usquebaughbaul, id est, usquebaugh, which at first taste affects all the members of the body: two spoonfuls of this last liquor is a sufficient dose; and if any man exceed this, it would presently... endanger his life. The trestarig and usquebaughbaul, are both made of oats.'

This is a potent reminder that the distillations of spirits was once a fairly hit and miss affair and that lethal – quite literally – brews were sometimes created. When alcoholic content reaches a certain level all spirits are lethal, but to the people of a small remote poverty stricken place like Lewis, a few drops of an extremely powerful spirit might have been one of the very few pleasures in otherwise unendingly hard lives.

ANCIENT TIPPLERS

Among the famous – and infamous – said to have drunk an ancient
version of whisky, a spirit distilled from grain anyway, are:

Alexander the Great
Alfred the Great
Charlemagne
Ghengis Khan
Tutankhamen

FIRE WATER

The toughness of Highland keepers is legendary, and even the more extraordinary stories of their antics are usually found to be true. A keeper from a very remote area was out early one winter morning getting his various bits and pieces ready for the first gentleman stalker of the season. He discovered that he needed some small item that was available in the nearest village three miles away, so he set off on foot knowing there was plenty of time as it was still very early in the morning. He would wake the shopkeeper who was a friend of his and be back before the gentleman was even out of bed.

At the edge of the village the keeper decided to stop for a wee dram when he saw that an old friend was already working in his garden. He stopped to talk to the man and after a few moments accepted the offer of a glass of whisky. He knocked it back, talked for a few more minutes and then carried on towards the village. About 10 minutes after he'd left, the keeper's friend realised that by mistake he'd given his friend a glass from the wrong stone jar. Instead of the jar which contained the whisky, he'd pulled out the jar filled with vitriol – sulphuric acid. The cottager was in agonies thinking his friend would probably die. He stood in the road waiting and hoping that the keeper would pass by on his way back to the estate, but no one came and in despair the cottager returned to his house to await the call of the police.

A few days later the cottager, still in an agony over the incident, saw his friend the keeper striding along the lane and he ran out to greet him. Before the cottager could say a word, the keeper shouted: 'Dugald! That was fine whisky ye gave me the other day – do you have more of it?'

The cottager could not believe his ears.

'Did you not feel bad after the whisky I gave you?'

'I canna remember tasting better whisky in my life,' said the keeper, smiling. 'Although there was one odd thing about it,' he continued. 'Every time I sneezed after drinking it I burned a hole in my handkerchief!'

BUTT WHERE'S THE WHISKY?

A Scottish fisherman fed up with having to give nips of his favourite whisky away to any and everyone he met while out fishing devised a cunning way around the problem. He went to the local tackle maker and repairer and asked him to hollow out the lower part of the butt of one of his salmon rods. This was to be filled with a narrow, specially made pewter tube with a screw top at one end – about the size of a very long fat cigar. The fisherman was delighted with the result. His rod looked just as it had always looked and it took just a moment to unscrew a special button on the rod handle to reveal the long, thin hip-flask.

How he was going to enjoy fishing with his secret supply! But imagine his horror when the first angler he met said: 'I hear Angus made you a special hip-flask to fit in your rod butt. Could I have a look at it over a dram or two?!'

The fisherman was outraged and remembered that he'd forgotten to swear the tackle maker to secrecy!

I'LL HAVE AN ISLAY

Distilleries on the small island of Islay, west Scotland:

Ardbeg
Bowmore
Bruichladdich
Bunnahabhain
Caol Ila
Lagavulin
Laphroaig
Kilchoman

DRAM-ATIC WRITING

'Is it the sarmon?' exclaimed the landlady. 'I can't say but it was rasonable; but the prayers is mighty unasy. It's no small a matter for a body in their fifty-nint' year to be moving so much in church. Mr. Grant sames a godly man, any way, and his garrel a hommble on; and a devout. Here, John, is a mug of cider, laced with whiskey. An Indian will drink cider, though he niver be athirst. 'I must say,' observed Hiram, with due deliberation, 'that it was a tongney thing; and I rather guess that it gave considerable satisfaction, There was one part, though, which might have been left out, or something else put in; but then I s'pose that, as it was a written discourse, it is not so easily altered as where a minister preaches without notes.'

James Fenimore Cooper, *The Pioneers*

DRAM-ATIC WRITING

'Who's drunk? I? No, no, captain! That won't do. You ought to know by this time the chief ain't free-hearted enough to make a sparrow drunk, b'gosh. I've never been the worse for liquor in my life; the stuff ain't made yet that would make me drunk. I could drink liquid fire against your whisky peg for peg, b'gosh, and keep as cool as a cucumber. If I thought I was drunk I would jump overboard – do away with myself, b'gosh. I would! Straight! And I won't go off the bridge. Where do you expect me to take the air on a night like this, eh? On deck amongst that vermin down there? Likely– ain't it! And I am not afraid of anything you can do.'

Joseph Conrad, *Lord Jim*

QUOTE UNQUOTE

Does whisky count as beer?
Homer Simpson

AN AFRICAN BOY IN THE HIGHLANDS

In the 1890s, when an orphaned African boy was brought to Scotland by James Grant, the owner of the Glen Grant Distillery at Rothes, a curious cross-culture legend began. Biawa, as the boy was known, was a member of the Kalanga tribe but he was to spend his long life in the Highlands of Scotland.

At Glen Grant House, Biawa became a pageboy, then later Major Grant's footman. In 1916, he enlisted in the Northampton Regiment and fought with the Mesopotamia Expeditionary Force fighting the Turks. Demobbed in March 1920, he returned to Glen Grant where he developed a passion for football – and whisky. He was a keen supporter of the local team, Rothes, and became such a fixture at the ground that he was given a complimentary seat and if the team played away from home, he travelled on the team bus.

When the Major died in 1931, Biawa stayed on to work for the Major's daughter and in the 1960s the story of his life appeared in the local newspaper and he became something of a celebrity.

The Major's grandson and owner of the distillery, Douglas Mackessack, chose not to move to the family house, which was divided into flats and let out to distillery workers and to Biawa, who died in Aberlour Hospital in 1972. No one knew his age, but he left all his money – £36.11 – to his favourite football club.

BEST CELLARS

Four books about whisky whose titles betray
their authors' devotion to the stuff:

My Love Affair with Whisky
Whisky Made Me
God Save Whisky
Whisky is Proof that God Exists

THE HARD STUFF

What makes whisky taste like whisky?
Answer on page 153.

ONE THAT GOT AWAY

No one really knows why the king of fish – the salmon – takes a bait in freshwater at all. Salmon are caught on spinners – bright pieces of metal that twirl and flash in the water – as well as on worms and artificial flies that look nothing at all like any real fly anyone has ever seen. They are also caught on prawns and maggots and minnows – yet no salmon has ever been caught and discovered to have anything in its stomach. The truth is that a salmon cannot eat in freshwater because it is to all intents and purposes a sea fish that comes to freshwater merely to breed – it does its feeding at sea.

Imagine then the astonishment of the Scottish angler who 'hooked' a huge salmon while fishing for minnows using an old whisky bottle lowered (using an equally old salmon rod and line) into a deep river pool. The idea was that the bait at the bottom of the whisky bottle would attract minnows in through the narrow neck of the bottle and the fisherman would then be able to lift the bottle out of the water complete with its cargo of minnows before the little fish could escape back out through the narrow neck of the bottle.

On this particular occasion he lowered his baited bottle into the deep river pool, waited for 20 minutes and then reeled in gradually. As the bottle reached the surface a salmon appeared, as if from nowhere, and grabbed the neck of the bottle just at the point where the line was tied to it. After a short battle – the fish was, after all, not hooked – the salmon had the sense to let go, but the mystery of this particular one that got away is: why on earth did it make a grab for a whisky bottle in the first place? Was this simply a particularly spirited fish?!

GOOGLEWHISKY

The World Wide Web lists 6,610,000 sites that feature the word whisky. These include:

Whisky as an aphrodisiac

Whisky sausages

Whisky lore

Whisky and the Taliban

Whisky and the surgeon's knife

Whisky for home decorators

STRANGER ON THE SHORE

A curious almost ghostly tale is still told in certain parts of North Yorkshire. It concerns two old men who had fished together for years down on an estuary where the sea met the river.

On the day in question they'd spent the morning repairing their house which stood alone, bleached and whitened by centuries of wind and salt. Then, having repaired the weatherboarding with odd planks that they found washed up on the beach, they decided to go fishing.

They tramped down to the water's edge, cast out their lines and waited. The thick cane rod tops nodded gently towards the water keeping time with the movement of the waves, but no fish disturbed their rhythm. Then they heard a voice: 'Anything doing?' The owner of the voice wore clothes that appeared to be made from a million layers of rags and scarves and tatters of old coats and jackets. He was almost emaciated, to judge by his face, but he wore so many layers of clothing, he looked like a giant.

'Anything doing?' he said again. Then: 'Give a poor man a drink and you'll catch a fish. Perhaps it's not such a good day for fishing. Perhaps you should be home by the fire, with the doors locked against the wind.' Then he said: 'Try casting that bit closer into the gullies where the poor fish lie to escape the coldest waves.'

They did as he said and amazingly started to catch fish. They passed him their flask filled with whisky and they caught even more fish. When they next looked around the tramp – if tramp he was – had gone, along with their whisky – and after that they never caught another fish.

DID YOU KNOW?

- The alcoholic strength of Scotch whisky used to be tested with gunpowder.

- One and a half ounces of whisky contains 104 calories – less than half a pint of beer or a glass of wine.

- A hot whisky toddy was long thought to be a cure for the common cold.

- A dram can apply only to a measure of Scotch whisky.

- 'The real McCoy' phrase was originally coined in reference to Scotch whisky smuggled into the USA during Prohibition by Captain Bill McCoy.

- Queen Victoria enjoyed whisky in her tea.

- The spring water source in the island of Islay flows through rock over 800 million years old (see page 81 for the island's whiskies).

INGREDIENTS FOR SUCCESS

Highland Cooler

2 drams of Scotch
2 dashes of Angostura
1 tsp of powdered sugar
Juice of half a lemon
Ice
Ginger ale

DRAM-ATIC WRITING

'To set the more obvious injustices right, and so to pave the way for a reform. Now look at that man digging in the field. I know him. He can neither read nor write, he is steeped in whisky, and he has as much intelligence as the potatoes that he is digging. Yet the man has a vote, can possibly turn the scale of an election, and may help to decide the policy of this empire. Now, to take the nearest example, here am I, a woman who have had some education, who have traveled, and who have seen and studied the institutions of many countries. I hold considerable property, and I pay more in imperial taxes than that man spends in whisky, which is saying a great deal, and yet I have no more direct influence upon the disposal of the money which I pay than that fly which creeps along the wall. Is that right? Is it fair?'

Arthur Conan Doyle, *Beyond the City*

The Colombian Tourist Board is probably the smallest of its kind in the world, largely because the country has such a reputation that only the brave would even consider taking a holiday there. For many it is a country where the feral adult male runs wild – no one takes any notice of the laws, least of all as they relate to whisky.

If you live in Bogotá you can buy all the world's great brands of whisky for a pittance – the only thing is they are all contraband. Conservative estimates reckon that more than 95% of Colombian whisky is sold outside the legitimate, taxed system. The police occasionally make a few raids, but are bought off or simply give up in the face of overwhelming odds. Where almost everyone breaks the law – including the police – what is the point of trying to enforce it?

But the Colombians adore whisky – and will do almost anything to get it. If the label says 'Johnnie Walker' they are happy, even though they know it is likely to have reached them via some very unsavoury process.

In a surprise move the Colombian government eventually took whisky manufacturers Diageo to court claiming that Colombia's drug barons, gangs of bandits and killers and complete disregard for the law could not be blamed entirely for the millions of dollars in lost revenue caused by illegal whisky consumption.

The case was heard in the United States and the Colombian government claimed that: 'The defendants (Diageo and several other international companies) have, at the highest corporate level, determined that it will be part of their operating business plan to sell their liquor products to and through criminal organisations and to accept criminal proceeds in payment by secret and surreptitious means.'

The Colombian government also accused Diageo et al of helping the drug barons. But for many, the case bore all the hallmarks of the Colombian government's latest attempt to blame outsiders for its internal problems; in the past, similar court action had been taken against international tobacco companies.

Diageo defended itself by insisting that it cooperated fully with the government and did not condone illicit sales to unofficial groups. The Colombian government failed to prove that this was not true, but no doubt they will be back again as the situation in their own country grows ever more desperate. Meanwhile, Colombians – when they are not kidnapping or shooting at each other – continue to enjoy their whisky at considerably reduced prices.

Cask-conditioned was never meant to be like this!

WHAT'S IN A NAME?

The correct pronunciation of whisky names

Whisky	Pronunciation
Auchentoshan	*Ochentoshen*
Bruichladdich	*Brew-ich-laddie*
Bunnahabhain	*Boon-a-havun*
Dailuaine	*Dall-Yewan*
Drumguish	*Drum-oo-ish*
Glenmorangie	*Glen-mo-r'nje (rhymes with Orangie)*
Knockdhu	*Nock-doo*
Laphroaig	*La-froyg*
Pittyvaich	*Pitt-ee-vay-ich*
Tullibardine	*Tully-bard-eye-n*

ONE FOR THE ROAD

Reports of whisky-related transport accidents in Scottish newspapers in the 1850s:

'Fell off while riding on the side of a wagon in a state of intoxication.'

'Skull broken while riding on top of a carriage – he was found with an empty bottle of whisky in his pocket.'

'Injured, jumped out after his hat having drunk too much whisky.'

BEST MEDICINE

JW Robertson Scott, who founded the *Countryman* magazine in 1927, was a deeply religious and fiercely teetotal Scot. His office deep in the Oxfordshire countryside was also his home and however much he loved his contributors – and some, like HE Bates, he loved very much indeed – he would not let them drink nor go with them for lunch if they insisted on going to the local pub.

Scott had grown up in Scotland at a time when drunkenness and the violence associated with it was everywhere and he had early on taken the pledge not to drink at all. In fact Scott had never tasted anything alcoholic until one eventful day in the *Countryman* office just after the war. A contributor had called on Scott to discuss an illustration for the cover of the magazine. It was a freezing cold day and the contributor, knowing Scott's hatred of drink, had transferred the contents of his usual hip-flask into an old cough mixture bottle.

Halfway through his discussions with Scott he excused himself, pulled out the bottle and took a sip, telling Scott that he had to take his medicine regularly as he was suffering from a chest infection.

It happened that Scott was similarly afflicted and he asked if he could try the contributor's medicine. The contributor, fearing this would be the end of his association with the magazine, handed the bottle over. Scott took a sip, made a note of the brand and handed the bottle back. The conversation continued as if nothing had happened.

The contributor was baffled until he remembered that Scott had never tasted any kind of alcohol and clearly had no idea that what he'd drunk was whisky. The contributor was very amused to receive a letter a few weeks later from Scott who said: 'I bought some of that medicine you let me try. My bottle was not nearly as effective as yours!'

It is said that keepers and gillies are traditionally fond of a drink, but this would rarely develop into alcoholism, probably because a drunken keeper would soon be an unemployed keeper. Similar constraints, for obvious reasons, have not applied to members of the landowning aristocracy.

Lord Massereene and Ferrard, for example, who owned an estate in County Antrim, in the north of Ireland, found that as he grew older his enthusiasm for sport declined as his fondness for alcohol increased. He was apparently quite a decent employer by the standards of the time and his keepers and beaters must have enjoyed the shoot rituals he established.

Massereene would get a household servant to bring out a table and a chair. These would be placed on the lawn in front of the house. Massereene would sit at the table with a row of bottles in front of him containing brandy, rum, gin and whisky. He would then line his beaters up in front of him, and each beater was given a number. In crisp autocratic tones, Massereene would then begin: 'Number one. Now, what'll you have?'

'I'll be quite happy with whatever your Lordship chooses,' Number one – well versed in the routine – would reply.

'Well now,' came his Lordship's reply, 'I should have said that brandy's the fellow for you.' He would then take the brandy bottle, pour a glass and drink it himself. 'Oh yes, definitely. That's your brandy,' he would say before selecting another glass, filling it and handing it to the beater. This ritual would be repeated until all the beaters had been offered whatever drink Massereene thought most suitable and of course for each drink he handed out, his lordship had one himself.

There seemed to be no logic to his Lordship's decision to award any one beater a particular drink. He chose at random and then reached for the appropriate bottle. Legend has it that Massereene, who was not a particularly keen shot, much preferred this early morning ritual to hanging about with a gun waiting for a few pheasants to fly over. It was also said that, on particularly big days when there were a great many beaters, his Lordship sometimes rolled gently off his chair after the 25th beater had drunk to his health.

QUOTE UNQUOTE

Wheat, noun: A cereal from which a tolerably good whisky can with some difficulty be made, and which is also used for bread.
Ambrose Bierce, from his *Devil's Dictionary*

The story of the Frongoch distillery – the first commercial whisky enterprise in Wales – is a fascinating one. It began in London's Hyde Park, in 1887 when two friends, Richard John Lloyd-Price and Robert Willis, discussed why Wales had no distillery. They decided to do something about it, and, having conducted water tests at the Tairvelyn Brook near Frongoch, Snowdonia, founded the Welsh Whisky Co in 1889 at Lloyd-Price's Rhiwlas Estate near Bala.

An experienced distiller from Scotland was soon brought in, and after Queen Victoria accepted a bottle in 1889, the company launched their Royal Welsh Whisky which must have been pretty good as it won top prize at the 1893 Chicago World Fair. A journalist from the *Liverpool Daily Courier* in 1892 described the Frongoch Distillery as follows:

'A noble building situated close to the Railway Station, and obvious therefore, as saying goes, to the meanest observer, although as yet the Directors of the Company have not considered it necessary to advertise its existence to the passing Railway traveller by painting any name or description upon its massive walls, erected as they are from the handsome and durable gray granite of the country.'

Despite launching a number of different brands – including the splendidly named Welsh Rare Bit – Frongoch had ceased production by 1900. The reason was probably the strong temperance movement in Wales and a number of bad batches of Frongoch whisky which spoiled its reputation. A few bottles of the whisky survive unopened including one owned by the Prince of Wales and kept at the Museum of Welsh Life.

WIT AND WHISKY

What is the difference between a battery and a whisky?
A battery has a negative side.

DICTIONARY MAN

'Come, let me know what it is that makes a Scotchman happy!'
(Samuel Johnson ordering for himself a glass of whisky.)
James Boswell, *Journal of a Tour to the Hebrides,* 1798

THE HARD STUFF

What did Robbie Burns do before he became known as a poet?
Answer on page 153.

COCKTAILS THAT INCLUDE WHISKY
AS THE MAIN INGREDIENT

Rattlesnake Shot • Red Dragon's Breath
Red Frog • Red Raider
Red Royal • Red Royal Shot
Red Snapper • Rooster Piss
Royal Butt • Royal Flush
Royal Peach • Royal Scandal
Ruby Slipper • Rusty Nail
Sax With T • Scoff-Law
Scotch Solace • Screaming Blue Viking
Smooth Sailing • Stone Fence

DRAM-ATIC WRITING

Passing through the narrow arch, I crossed the court-yard, the confined precincts of which were made visible by a lantern over the portal of the Province House. On entering the bar-room, I found, as I expected, the old tradition monger seated by a special good fire of anthracite, compelling clouds of smoke from a corpulent cigar. He recognized me with evident pleasure; for my rare properties as a patient listener invariably make me a favorite with elderly gentlemen and ladies of narrative propensities. Drawing a chair to the fire, I desired mine host to favor us with a glass apiece of whiskey punch, which was speedily prepared, steaming hot, with a slice of lemon at the bottom, a dark-red stratum of port wine upon the surface, and a sprinkling of nutmeg strewn over all. As we touched our glasses together, my legendary friend made himself known to me as Mr. Bela Tiffany; and I rejoiced at the oddity of the name, because it gave his image and character a sort of individuality in my conception. The old gentleman's draught acted as a solvent upon his memory, so that it overflowed with tales, traditions, anecdotes of famous dead people, and traits of ancient manners, some of which were childish as a nurse's lullaby, while others might have been worth the notice of the grave historian.

Nathaniel Hawthorne,
Legends of the Province House

Number of pages in Chambers Scotch Whisky, *by Michael Moss,* 91
and the year in the 1900s in which it was first published

DRINK ME

Five weird ad slogans:

1971 Johnnie Walker Black Label
'It will make your father proud just to know you can afford it.'

1971 White Horse Whisky
'You can take a white horse anywhere.'

1971 Chivas Regal
'You either have it... or you don't.'

1997 Glenlivet
'Sure beats training the dog to fetch the newspaper.'
(uttered by a bird with a bottle in its claws)

2002 Jim Beam
'It ain't bragging when it's true.'

26 AROMAS

The bouquet of Glenmorangie Ten Years Old was investigated by a world-renowned French parfumier. He 'nosed' a grand total of 26 aromas, listed below, arguably a more complex combination than any other single malt Scotch whisky.

Algae • Almond • Ambergris
Apple • Bergamot orange • Cinnamon
Fruit stone • Genista • Gentian
Geranium • Ginger • Heather
Iodine • Lemon peel • Liquorice
Mango • Narcissus • Nutmeg
Peat • Peony • Pepper
Pine resin • Quince • Vanilla
Verbena • Wild mint

BEST SELLING

Quick stats about whisky

- Scotch whisky uses 425,000 tonnes of barley and around 542,000 tonnes of other cereal a year.

- Irish records show that in the late 1100s, distilling was first done in monasteries to produce medicine. And the Royal Exchequer Rolls of 1494 show the earliest Scottish record is of the sale of 500kg (1,102lb) of malt to a Friar John Corr, 'wherewith to make aqua vitae'.

DISAPPEARING ACT

When the licence duty was raised to 9d per gallon of whisky in 1797, legal distilleries disappeared completely from Campbeltown for 20 years.

QUOTE UNQUOTE

Tell me what brand of whiskey that Grant drinks.
I would like to send a barrel of it to my other generals.
Abraham Lincoln, US President

RECIPE FOR PICKLED HADDOCK

Amid the crisply drawn, boy's-own euphoria of Hergé's famous Tintin stories, it is easy to miss the spectre of Oliver Reed hanging over one of the main characters. However, a cursory glance at Captain Haddock's behaviour will reveal a major propensity for amusing bouts of whisky-fuelled disorientation.

This is down to Haddock's taste for the Loch Lomond label of central Scotland – a fine and glowing whisky, by all accounts, which happens to be every bit as real as the Captain isn't. This is despite some renowned 'Tintinologists' becoming so immersed in the fictional strength of Hergé's world that they overestimate the reach of his invention. For instance, in his book, *Tintin: The Complete Companion*, Michael Farr says: '[on his publisher's insistence], Hergé changed a very real Johnny Walker tanker to his own Loch Lomond. The result was a tanker-load of a less authentic tipple, the future Captain's Favourite.' Likewise, author Pierre Assouline dubbed Loch Lomond a 'fictitious brand'.

Such claims overlook Hergé's manic attention to detail. Two of his greatest achievements were that every vehicle in the Tintin canon had a real-life basis, and that any Chinese or Arabic writing seen on Tintin's travels actually made sense. What worked for cars and languages also worked for whisky. In *The Red Sea Sharks*, Haddock made some room for a change from his cause célèbre by accepting a bottle of Haig – a Scotch that few would dispute the existence of, much as they might rue it after a night's indulgence.

Any doubters should plot a course for www.lochlomond distillery.com, and find out what excited the Captain's thirst.

The Grant family is a name to be reckoned with in Scottish whisky history. Descended from John Grant, chief of the Grant clan in the mid sixteenth century, the family produced a number of interesting characters including Elizabeth Grant whose Victorian diaries recorded her life on Speyside in north-east Scotland. Elizabeth's diaries were published posthumously in 1898 as the *Memoirs of a Highland Lady*. Among Elizabeth's memories are numerous references to whisky and its role in the Highlanders' lives. At one point Elizabeth says: 'The dram was the Highland prayer, it began, accompanied, and ended all things.'

Elizabeth's memories of the visit to the Highlands in 1822 of King George IV (known as Georgie Porgie when Prince of Wales) produced this diary entry from Elizabeth: 'One incident connected with this time made me very cross. Lord Conyngham, the Chamberlain, was looking everywhere for pure Glenlivet whisky; the King drank nothing else. It was not to be had out of the Highlands. My father sent word to me – I was the cellarer – to empty my pet bin, where was whisky long in wood, long in uncorked bottles, mild as milk, and the true contraband goût in it. Much as I grudged this treasure it made our fortunes afterwards, showing on what trifles great events depend. The whisky, and 50 brace of ptarmigan all shot by one man,

went up to Holyrood House, and were graciously received and made much of, and a reminder of this attention at a proper moment by the gentlemanly Chamberlain ensured to my father the Indian judgeship.'

In the manner typical of Victorian aristocratic attitudes to the ordinary people, Elizabeth thought whisky was OK for her but bad for the common people: 'At every house it was offered, at every house it must be tasted or offence would be given, so we were taught to believe. I am sure now had we steadily refused compliance with so incorrect a custom it would have been far better for ourselves, and might all the sooner have put a stop to so pernicious a habit among the people. Whisky-drinking was and is the bane of that country; from early morning to late at night it went on. Decent gentlewomen began the day with a dram. In our house the bottle of whisky, with its accompaniment of a silver salver full of small glasses, was placed on the side-table with cold meat every morning. In the pantry a bottle of whisky was the allowance per day, with bread and cheese in any desired quantity, for such messengers or visitors whose errands sent them in that direction. The very poorest cottages could offer whisky; all the men engaged in the wood manufacture drank it in goblets three times a day, yet except at merry-making we never saw anyone tipsy.'

*Too much whisky might not be the
best thing for your complexion!*

WIT AND WHISKY

A guy is stranded on a desert isle, alone for 10 years. One day, he sees a speck on the horizon. He thinks, it's not a ship. The speck gets a little closer, and he thinks, it's not a boat. The speck gets even closer and he thinks, it's not a raft. Then, out of the surf comes a gorgeous blonde woman wearing a wet suit and scuba gear. She walks up to the guy, all Ursula Andress, and says: 'How long has it been since you've had a cigarette?'

'Ten years!' he says. She reaches over, unzips a waterproof pocket on her left sleeve and pulls out a pack of fresh cigarettes. He takes one, lights it, and says, 'Man, oh, man! Is that good!'

Then she asks: 'How long has it been since you've had a roast beef sandwich?' He replies: 'Ten years!' She reaches over, unzips her waterproof pocket on the right, pulls out a tasty sarnie, and gives it to him. He wolfs it down and says: 'Wow, that's fantastic!'

Then she starts unzipping this long zip that runs down to the front of her wet suit, and she says to him: 'How long has it been since you've had some REAL fun?' The man replies: 'My God! Don't tell me that you've got a bottle of Glenmorangie in there!'

Whisky is liquid sunshine.
George Bernard Shaw, playwright

YOU CAN DRINK IT FROM ANYTHING

- Illegal distillers liked to drink their whisky from kettles (in case the customs man turned up unexpectedly).

- Smugglers on shipboard often kept their drams in hollowed-out sticks that looked to all intents and purposes like a club.

- Priests used to regularly keep whisky in the spare wine cup during mass.

- Elderly Irish women with a taste for the amber nectar, but who wanted to seem ultra respectable (ie teetotal), were known to keep their whisky in the chamber pot!

WORLDWIDE WHISKY HUNT

Canadian whisky company, Canadian Club started an ingenious advertising campaign in 1967 that set whisky lovers on a treasure hunt. Organisers placed cases of the whisky in exotic locations around the world and gave clues to the public in the sports sections of newspapers. Cases were tucked away in such far-flung spots as Mount Kilimanjaro in Tanzania, Mount St Helens in the US, the Swiss Alps, Angel Falls in Venezuela and Death Valley in the US. The idea was that whoever found a case of the whisky won an all-expenses-paid round-the-world trip.

Some of the cases were found quite quickly – the one in Death Valley was discovered in just a week, but a case placed on top of a sky scraper in New York lay undetected for 13 weeks. And the one on Mount Kilimanjaro was not found until the mid 1970s when a Danish journalist stumbled upon it. Probably the most remote location was the Arctic and it proved to be too much as that particular case has never been found.

The campaign was a major coup from an advertising point of view, running for 21 years between 1967 and 1981, by which time 22 cases had been hidden. It is not known if the treasure hunters were more interested in the whisky or the round-the-world trip, but the organisers must have known a free case of whisky was enough to rouse anyone to join the hunt!

VICE PRESIDENTS OF THE US WHOSE MAIN TIPPLE WAS WHISKY

Alben W Barkley
John C Breckinridge
John Nance Garner
William A Wheeler

DRUNKEN BIRDS

In 1965 there was a short-lived series of incidents in which poachers, who would normally have used nets or light loads in light shotguns, turned to the skilled art of making pheasants drunk. One West Country poacher took a local journalist along to see how it was done. Before they left the poacher's cottage, the journalist saw how the poacher had soaked barley in water for a few days. Then the water was drained off and replaced with whisky. After a couple of hours the whisky had all been absorbed and the poacher and journalist set off for the woods.

The poacher explained that it was important to take a shotgun so that any passerby or rambler would simply assume that this was a man out for a walk along the hedgerows in search of a rabbit or two. Most people assume that a man with a shotgun and dressed in the right kind of gear is out shooting perfectly legally. 'It has a lot to do with the fact that they just assume you're a toff – once you've got them thinking that, you know they wouldn't dream of questioning you.'

When the two men reached the edge of a wood the poacher crouched down quickly and took about a pound of the whisky-laden barley grains from a big hidden inner pocket. These were left in a little pile and the poacher then laid a thin trail of single grains from the pile into the wood. As soon as this had been done the two men walked away from the barley trail on the edge of the wood and hid in a ditch from which they kept watch.

The journalist couldn't believe what happened next. At first a few pheasants appeared following the trail of barley grains. After another 20 minutes, more than a dozen pheasants were milling around the rapidly diminishing pile of grain, but one or two seemed decidedly unsteady on their feet. Yet another 20 minutes after that, several of the pheasants were squabbling and fighting each other. Others staggered around barely able to stand. One or two were flat on their backs apparently fast asleep. The poacher nodded at the journalist and it was a simple matter for them to cross the field and simply pick each pheasant up and put it in a sack.

As any aficionado will know, the water supply is crucial when producing a fine malt whisky. Glenmorangie Distillery knows just how important that is as their supply was nearly lost in the nineteenth century.

Today, Glenmorangie is distilled using water from the nearby Tarlogie Springs. However, in the 1800s, the water supply was owned by the Ross family of the Tarlogie estate on the outskirts of Tain. As Tain began to expand in the 1840s, a new water source was required. In 1851, the Tarlogie Springs were identified as the ideal solution to their growing needs. A delegation was sent to inspect the springs and came back with a glowing report; the Council minutes recorded that '...the Committee have not followed the stream throughout but have reason to believe that it flows to the sea past the great stone at Morangie and it is not appropriated to any useful purpose'.

Obviously the distillery and its ever loyal consumers disagreed with the Council's assessment! Fortunately for Glenmorangie drinkers, a full inquiry was launched by the Council and the springs were dismissed as a viable source for the town.

Andrew Maitland Snr, from a local architecture firm, was dispatched to cost and plan the tanks and pipes needed for a new water system. Fortuitously, the summer of 1851 was exceptionally dry and Mr Maitland reported that the springs were 'found to be much diminished and not to be calculated on for a permanent supply'. And so Tain looked elsewhere for water and Glenmorangie continued to put the unique water source to good use.

To protect this unique water supply Glenmorangie bought both the springs and the 650 surrounding acres from the Duke of Westminster's estate in 1989.

DRAM-ATIC WRITING

The Parkers, having children, had dined early, and he was sitting out on a little porch smoking his pipe, drinking whisky and water, and looking at the sea. His eldest girl was standing between his legs, and his wife, with the other three children round her, was sitting on the door-step. 'I've brought my wife to see you,' said Lopez, holding his hand to Mrs Parker, as she rose from the ground.

'I told her that you'd be coming,' said Sexty, 'and she wanted me to put off my pipe and little drop of drink; but I said that if Mrs Lopez was the lady I took her to be she wouldn't begrudge a hard-working fellow his pipe and glass on a holiday.'

Anthony Trollope, *The Prime Minister*

WHISKY IN FILM

Gone with the Wind, 1939

At one point Clarke Gable's character Rhett hands Mammy a glass of whisky. She sniffs it before taking a sip. Tea was supposed to have been in the glass, but Clarke Gable substituted real whisky as a joke.

Highlander, 1986

Christopher Lambert's character (Conner MacLeod) orders a Glenmorangie whisky in a bar. Unfortunately, he mispronounces the whisky's name.

Apparently all the extras got very drunk on whisky to keep warm during filming in the Highlands of Scotland. When you see the Scottish charge insanely, it is said to be because they were all drunk.

Titanic, 1997

When the Titanic begins to sink, a man in white is drinking whisky next to Leonardo DiCaprio and Kate Winslet's characters. This man actually existed on the actual ship; he drank whisky to keep warm and survived the ice.

PEPYS INTO THE PAST

When the great seventeenth-century diarist Samuel Pepys realised that he would have to have an operation for gallstones he immediately made his will. In those pre-anaesthetic days and with no awareness of the need for hygiene the chances of surviving such an operation were at best slim. The patient was strapped to a table and held down by half a dozen burly porters invited into the house for the purpose. The surgeon would then cut the patient in a line from anus and testicles. He would then grope about inside to find the stones and pull them out. The patient would then be roughly sewn up and cow's milk would be poured over the wound in an attempt to help it heal. Of course the most likely effect of the milk would be to make the wound fester; the patient would get gangrene and die in agony.

This didn't happen to Pepys who was lucky to need his surgery at the beginning of the period in which the patient was given whisky to drink to ease the pain – but whisky was also poured over the wound. It hurt like hell but it effectively cleansed the wound and dramatically increased the patient's chances of survival – the doctors had no idea why this was happening, but whisky's reputation as a panacea for all ills no doubt gave some wily doctor the idea of doing it and the practice spread.

What better than whisky to bridge the social divide!

G-SPOTS

Gauger – An old name for the exciseman, whose job it was to stop illicit distillation and smuggling.

Grain whisky – Whisky made by a continuous distilling method, usually made up from either wheat or maize. Used to blend with a straight whisky.

Green malt – Malt that has been soaked in water and started germinating, but has not yet gone through the kilning (heating) stage.

Grist – Malt that has been ground.

For decades at the end of the eighteenth century and well into the nineteenth, the battle between excisemen and illegal distillers and whisky smugglers continued in Scotland. The tax on legitimate whisky pushed it way beyond the means of ordinary men, so illegal distilling, whatever the penalty, continued since many saw the tax as illegal – or at least immoral – in the first place.

Highlanders who had made their whisky were reluctant to throw away their homemade stills just because the King of England told them to. Illegal whisky production only really began to disappear when a more equitable system of taxation was found and rising prosperity lessened the necessity for illegal distillation.

The means by which the illegal distillers dealt with the authorities is fascinating. At a Justice of the Peace Court at Stornoway, on the Isle of Lewis, during 1808-1810, the records show that the crofters regularly paid stiff fines for illegally making whisky, but whenever a man was fined in this way the fine would always be paid by a group of families who clearly worked together and had come to an agreement to protect each other from the law. Once the fines had been paid the distilling families got straight back to work.

The illegal distillers were also masters at avoiding getting caught – stills were concealed under bracken and ferns or they were set up in caves or in pits dug beneath the crofters' houses; lookouts were posted when the stills were operating and of course the wily Highlanders knew their territory far better than the excisemen. If anything untoward was spotted, all trace of distilling activity vanished in an instant. Distillers were sometimes caught, but often as a result of details given by an enemy with whom a particular family had been feuding rather than by skilful detective work. And of course the excisemen were easy to bribe since many – like Robbie Burns, later to achieve immortality as a poet – were sympathetic to the whisky men.

Perhaps the remains of long-forgotten stills lie hidden in caves and buried under peat mounds throughout the Highlands to this day. But the clearances – carried out by clan leaders educated in England and remembered with bitterness to this day – killed the ancient Highlanders' way of life, and the huge network of illegal whisky manufacture vanished. Where once tens of thousands of poor crofters had eked out a living with only their whisky for profit and entertainment, by the late 1800s the land was populated only by sheep.

But traces of the old ways do survive though we can no longer see them. It is said that at the bottom of perhaps hundreds of small lochs dotted about the Highlands and islands lie the ghostly remains of small, illegal stills, thrown into the waters to avoid detection or when at last the family was driven off their land.

HIGH-SPEED LAWYERS

There's a story recorded in the British *Railway Times* from the early part of the twentieth century that shows the palliative effects of whisky under, quite literally, the most trying of circumstances.

It concerns four elderly judges who had been sent from London as a Special Commission to try some rioters at Stafford, central England, and who decided to take the special train from London's Euston station. None of them had ever travelled by rail before and they were at best apprehensive, at worst terrified. All had said special goodbyes to their families and had checked their wills and that their affairs were in order before setting out. Each had also provided himself with a hip-flask filled with whisky, for they were all members not just of the judiciary, but also of the long-vanished Whisky Club.

Lord Abinger, presiding in the Court of Exchequer, on hearing that the judges had travelled by rail said they were foolish to allow themselves to be propelled through the air at a speed for which God had not designed the human body. Even if he were called as a witness, he insisted, and compelled to attend the court, he would refuse to travel by rail whatever the risk of prosecution for contempt of court.

In the event the judges survived the journey but they found the experience of travelling at speeds in excess of 30 miles per hour so exhilarating that they could think of nothing else for weeks afterwards. Such were their high spirits that the rioters were let off with far more lenient sentences than would otherwise have been the case.

QUOTE UNQUOTE

My God, so much I like to drink Scotch that sometimes I think my name is Igor Stra-whiskey.
Igor Stra-whi... er, Stravinsky, Russian composer

DOES MY BUTT LOOK BIG IN THIS?

Barrel Type	Approximate Content in Litres
Butt	500
Hogshead	250-305
American Barrel	173-191
Quarter	127-159
Octave	45-68

BEST SELLING

Quick stats about whisky sales

- Glenmorangie is the best-selling brand of single malt whisky in Scotland.

- 30 bottles of Scotch whisky are sold overseas every second.

- 88.4 million cases of whisky were sold worldwide in 2004. They would stretch 16,807 miles – three times the distance between Edinburgh and Shanghai – if they were laid end to end.

- In recent years whisky has been exported to about 200 different markets all over the world. The major markets are the European Union, USA, Japan and other Asian markets.

THE HARD STUFF

Which is the odd one out: Glenlivet, Glenmorangie or Glendalough?
Answer on page 153.

DRAM-ATIC WRITING

On our way to Peterhead we stopped at the pretty village of Old Deer to inspect its little Distillery. The village is pleasantly situated in a plain, on the south banks of the Deer River. The surrounding country is ornamented with woods and plantations, and there are heath-covered ridges in all directions. Near the village are to be seen the ruins of the Abbey of Deer, built in the thirteenth century by the good Earl of Buchan, for some monks of the Cistercian order; from the appearance of the remains it must have been a very extensive building. There are also, in the vicinity, four Druidical temples, that at Biffie being the most conspicuous, and an object of great interest to antiquarians.

The Lowlands of Aberdeenshire are good grain-growing districts, hence the establishment of Distilleries and Breweries in this neighbourhood. The Glenadon Distillery was built in the year 1845, by Messrs. Milne & Co.,' the farmer proprietors of the Biffie Brewery close by. It is a nice little compact work, but too small for us to enter into detail, suffice it to say, that the water used comes from the Biffie springs, in a glen same 200 feet above the level of the Distillery, and that home-grown barley only is used. The Whisky is pure Malt, and the annual output is 12,000 gallons. In addition to the Distillery, Messrs. Geo. J. Wilson and Co. are now also the owners of the Biffie Brewery.

Alfred Barnard, *The Whisky Distilleries of the United Kingdom*, 1887

WHISKY AFICIONADOS

Whisky lover	Most-loved whisky
Iain Banks, British writer	Laphroaig
Sammy Davis Jr, American entertainer	J&B Rare
Michael Douglas, American actor	Macallan
Edward VII, British King	Glendullan
Duke Ellington, American musician	Johnnie Walker, Red Label
Dean Martin, American entertainer	J&B Rare
Dorothy Parker, American writer	White Horse
Prince Charles, British heir to the throne	Laphroaig
John Simpson, British journalist	Ardberg

QUOTE UNQUOTE

*Whiskey has killed more men than bullets, but most men
would rather be full of whiskey than bullets.*
Logan Pearsall Smith, writer

SALT AND PEPPER

Mr Salt was one of a group of railway traffic officers who looked after railway freight at a time when the railway companies were starting to take business away from middlemen carriers like Pickfords, who had been carriers by road and canal for centuries.

The Midland Railway employed Mr Salt as well as a manager, based at Leeds, called Mr Pepper. At various railway meetings of the day there were inevitable jokes as to Pepper and Salt being mustered.

Mr Salt was famous for his love of whisky – he never seemed to be drunk, but he drank small amounts of whisky almost continually. He was also a man with a very gloomy, cadaverous countenance and when the directors of the railway company wanted a carriage kept free (for whatever reason) during a journey they would ask Mr Salt to tie up his head with a handkerchief, grasp 'a large bottle of whisky as if it were life-saving medicine' and sit by a window.

Mr Salt looked so close to death when he took his seat that unwanted members of the public peering into his compartment were too terrified to attempt to sit in it.

MEDICINAL PURPOSES

There are very few first-hand accounts of what it felt like to travel by rail at the very dawn of the railway era. But one man – a Mr Fergusson of Woodhill, Edinburgh – described the strangeness of a mode of transport that, at the time, must have felt pretty much like space travel today. In a note written just a day or so after the events described, he wrote of the journey from Manchester to Liverpool in the UK:

'We started with eight carriages attached to the engine with such imperceptible motion, that it was only when I found myself unable to read a milestone, or to distinguish the features of those who darted past in the opposite direction, that I was led to consult my watch for the rate of travelling; when I found, to my astonishment, that the next five miles were done in fifteen minutes.

'Such was the rapidity of our journey that my fellow passengers, apprehensive to a man, had armed themselves with various bottles of strong drink and hip-flasks. Whisky seemed the favoured antidote to the ferocity of our journey and one elderly man confided to me that he had been too terrified to travel at all by train until he had been assured by a medical practitioner of his acquaintance that the cure for fear of travel

was three good lugs of a very good whisky. Cheaper blends, he explained to me, would not do the trick since their purity was not up to the settling qualities demanded by high-speed travel.

'My friend's fear of travelling sober can be well understood when one considers that from the powers of the locomotive engines on the railroad, goods and passengers are conveyed from Liverpool to Manchester, a distance of 32 miles, in an astonishing two hours.

'Among other regulations, a watchman is stationed permanently on the line every half mile to detect any stone or other dangerous impediment upon the rail. As he sees the carriages approaching, if there is a difficulty, he stops and extends his arm in sufficient time to enable the engineer to stop the train.

'As we bowled along, a little circumstance, more ludicrous than dangerous, occasioned a small loss of time. The hook by which No. 2 carriage was attached to No. 1 suddenly gave way, and the engine, with one carriage only, shot off like lightning, leaving the others to follow as they best could. The alarm was, however, quickly given, the engine reversed its movement, and the whole affair was speedily adjusted.'

WAITING FOR WHISKY

When HRH Prince Andrew opened the Glenmorangie Distillery Museum, in Tain in the Scottish Highlands, in July 1997, the company presented him with his own special cask of Glenmorangie. The cask continues to mature at the distillery and won't be ready until 2007 – just in time for his parents' 60th wedding anniversary.

COCKTAILS THAT INCLUDE WHISKY AS THE MAIN INGREDIENT

Canadian Bull • Canadian Hunter
Capital Punishment • Catfish
Celtic Spirit • Cherry MacGregor
Coffee Grinder • CoonDogg
Crazy Moose • Crown and Choke
Crystal Virgin • Curtain Call
Damned If You Do
Dirty Irish Whiskey
Double Jack • Dublin Doubler
Duck Fart

DRAM-ATIC WRITING

William Grant, of the Balvenie Distillery, was a man of extraordinary capacities. One of the Dufftown Volunteers, William Ramsay, gave a vivid portrait of the old Major:

'Mr Grant was always busy with something. Oh yes, he was a very bright man – a very live cove. He wasn't a particularly tall man but he was a broad man that could carry himself, and always with dignity – nothing proud about him.'

Although he spoke in the broad Scots of his native Banffshire the Major had a withering command of English particularly when he had a pen in his hand. Highly efficient himself and consumed with energy and ambition he found it difficult to countenance incompetence in others and his bluntness was legendary. On the other hand, with his staff he was a model of consideration. The story goes that he always whistled loudly when he moved around the distillery, especially when approaching a warehouse where he might have stumbled on one of the workers extracting a dram from a convenient cask.

William Grant remained active in the company until his death in 1923 at the grand age of 83.

HL MacKenzie, *Whisky*, 1928

A DRAM FOR THE GILLIE

For the salmon and trout fisherman whisky is part and parcel of the pleasure of being on the water, rod in hand. There are very few game fishermen who don't drink whisky and the gillie who refuses a dram is a creature who has never existed.

A famous Victorian gillie who regularly took a rich American fishing on a famous Scottish river, quickly realised that despite his client's obvious wealth the man did not realise that it is the worst possible social error not to offer one's gillie a wee dram at regular intervals throughout the fishing day.

Now as the gillie is effectively a servant – though a rather special one – it's very difficult for him to complain. On the other hand a gillie without his dram is not likely to make the greatest effort on behalf of a particular client – this particular gillie found it increasingly difficult even to be civil to the man.

Eventually the American hooked a big fish and as it approached the net the gillie deliberately slipped and knocked the fish off the line – 'I'm sorry but my nerves are bad,' said the gillie, 'I've been teetotal all day.' The American took the hint and on subsequent days relations between the two were restored. But the American never hooked another fish.

NOT SO FAMOUS WHISKY BOOK TITLES

Whisky and the Stars

A Lifetime Among Malts

Sociological Perspectives on The Cult of Whisky

A Hit! A Hit! Why Whisky Makes My Blood Boil

God's View of the Distilling Trade or
Why the Lord Knows Whisky is Sinful

WHISKY EATS

Atholl Brose Pudding
Serves 4

$\frac{1}{2}$ pint double cream, 3fl oz whisky, 3tbsp runny heather honey, 2oz toasted pinhead oatmeal.

Whip cream until it holds shape, stir in oatmeal and honey. Chill, and mix in whisky just before serving.

IT'LL PUT A SMILE ON YOUR FACE

In Uruguay, people don't say 'cheese' to force a smile for the camera, they say 'whisky'. Apparently just the thought of whisky is enough to bring a smile to anyone's lips!

DELANEY'S LIQUID TREASURE

Whisky's more mysterious aspects, bound up in antiquity and jealously guarded secrets, give rise to many lasting legends – and in Australia, few exponents are more legendary than 1880s bootlegger, Tom Delaney.

The Irishman operated in the Nirranda region of Victoria, where he kept a DIY distillery in a shanty house. He was said to have produced up to 100 gallons a week, and eventually ran afoul of authorities by putting his own copies of the government's official seal on his bottles. He was tracked down by ace excise detective John Christie – an attaché to HRH Prince Alfred, former boxing champion and master of disguise. After Christie sprung his shack, Delaney became a fugitive, but finally gave himself up in late 1893. However, he was thought to have buried a large portion of his existing stock somewhere in Nirranda, which has provided modern-day whisky fans with a tantalising treasure hunt.

In early 2004, a local group called Whisky Stills, comprised of firewater enthusiasts and some of Delaney's descendants, campaigned to have the most likely burial site, an intersection off Great Ocean Road called Delaney's Corner, turned into a tourist attraction – complete with information signs and a 'whisky drive' guiding visitors to key Delaney locations. At the time, Whisky Stills' chairman, Alan Hart, spoke of the area's attraction:

'They reckon there's some whisky out in the flat paddock... We know the first Delaney was caught early on, but Tom was going flat out through the 1880s and 1890s, making his own moonshine. Apparently it was a pretty good brew – pretty strong. There could be ten, fifty, sixty demijohns full of whisky out there – who knows? Someone dug up a hole a few years ago, but I think they were in the wrong spot.'

QUOTE UNQUOTE

*Always carry a flagon of whiskey in case of snakebite,
and furthermore, always carry a small snake.*
WC Fields, comedian and whisky aficionado

OUR GLENS

I love Scotland Glens, and whatever else we lose,
Please leave us our Glens, our glorious Glens
Our mountains are grand, Ben Lomond, Ben Nevis too,
You can have all these Bens, but leave us our Glens.

Glenfiddich, Glenlivet, Glendronach, Glen Grant
Can you do without them, if you must know, I can't
Put a drop in a glass of Glen Grant or Glen Drottar
It's a perfectly bearable way to drink water

Take our Highland Schottishe, or marches, strathspeys and reels,
Take our old Scottish Waltz, but leave us our malts,
Remove if you will our Ladies conveniences,
And our Gentlemens, but leave us our Glens

Glenfarclas, Glen Lochy, Glen Garioch, Glen Faul
I once knew a man who had sampled them all
Glen Ugie, Glenkinchie, Glen Isla, that's plenty
He looked 65, but in fact he was 20.

I'd willingly lose our culture, or most of it,
Including that mess called Full Highland Dress
With the whole ethnic bit, with haggis and Hogmanay
I'd gladly dispense, but leave us our Glens

Glenturret, Glen Scotia and last week Glen Fyne
Was rare at communion when we ran out of wine
Glenglassoch, Glen Lossie, Glendullan Glenmorangie
I prefer them to Cointreau which I find too orangey.

So breathes there a Scot whose views and priorities
When laid on the line are different from mine
Take our jobs, take our homes, take anything else you will
Wife, family and friends, but leave us our Glens

Glenfiddich, Glenlivet, Glendronach, Glen Grant
Can you do without them, if you must know, I can't
Put a drop in a glass of Glen Grant or Glen Drottar
It's a perfectly bearable way to drink water.

Buff Hardie and James McDonald

PROOF POSITIVE

How the US and Europe compare when it comes to alcoholic content

American	British and European
100% Proof	50% Alc. vol.
86% Proof	43% Alc. vol
80% Proof	40% Alc. vol.

WHISKY IN FILM

The Ladykillers, 1955
This hit prompted the *Daily Express* to claim: 'aside from Scotch whisky, Mr Alec Guinness is the best export to America we have got.'

Tunes of Glory, 1960
Alex Guinness plays Major Jock Sinclair, who says: 'Whisky for the gentlemen that like it. And for the gentlemen that don't like it – Whisky.'

The Power and the Glory, 1961
This flick, based on Graham Greene's novel, has Laurence Olivier playing a 'whisky priest' in post-revolution Mexico.

Unforgiven, 1992
Clint Eastwood's Oscar winning western. The film was set in the town of Big Whisky.

Shanghai Noon, 2000
During one scene in this Jackie Chan western, one character drinks from a bottle of whisky outside a saloon. He puts the bottle down and you can see that the cork is still on the bottle. Then the horse that is right beside him picks it up to drink the rest of it.

DRINK DRIVING

It is an astonishing fact, but a fact nonetheless, that until the end of the steam era, train drivers were allowed to drink alcohol before – sometimes even while – driving. It was simply assumed that no driver would overdo it because that would put both his life and those of his passengers at risk. The remarkable safety record of the steam era tends to suggest that allowing drivers and firemen to police their own drinking really did work. Which explains why no one batted an eyelid when in winter a driver would be spotted in his open (and freezing) cab sipping from a hip-flask before setting off into the icy morning.

QUOTE UNQUOTE

*Giving money and power to government is like giving
whiskey and car keys to teenage boys.*
PJ O'Rourke, writer

SCOTCH HIGHS AND LOWS

Lowland malt whiskies are made south of an invisible line from
Dundee in the east to Greenock in the west.

Highland malt whiskies come from anywhere north of that line.

Malts from Speyside are Highland malts, but they are so distinctive
they come into a group of their own.

Malts from Islay are in a class of their own.

DRINKING TO THE FUTURE

**When Cleopatra's Needle was erected on London's Thames
Embankment at the end of the nineteenth century, the following
items are said to have been buried beneath it:**

A model of the hydraulic equipment used to raise the obelisk

A two-foot rule

A child's feeding bottle and some toys

A tin of hairpins

Some tobacco

A portrait of Queen Victoria

A collection of newspapers

Photographs of women

Two bottles of Scottish whisky

WHAT DO THEY MEAN?

English translations of famous Scottish whisky names include:

Ardbeg ....small headland
Bruichladdich ....the bank of the shore
Bunnahabhain...foot or bottom of the river
Caol Islay ....narrow island sound
Lagavulin ....hollow by the mill
Laphroaig......................................beautiful hollow by the broad bay
Glenmorangie..valley of peace

In the early 1790s the *Old Statistical Account of Scotland* was published. This paints a fascinating portrait of a Scotland that no longer exists; it mentions customs and traditions that reveal what an extraordinary world we have lost.

In the parish of Borrowstownness in Linlithgow, for example, the Reverend Robert Rennie found the love of spirits objectionable: 'The walks about the town, are romantic and inviting; the walks on the quays, and on the west beach are, at all times, dry and pleasant, much fitted to promote health and longevity. But here, as in many other places specified in the *Old Statistical Account of Scotland*, tippling houses are too numerous. It may be seriously regretted, by the friends of religion and virtue, that so many people are licensed to vend ardent spirits in every town and village. Such places ensnare the innocent, become the haunts of the idle and dissipated, and ruin annually the health and morals of thousands of mankind. Perhaps, if the malt-tax were abolished, and an adequate additional tax laid upon British spirits, as in the days of our fathers, malt-liquor would be produced, to nourish and strengthen, instead of whisky, which wastes and enfeebles the constitution: Or, were Justices of the Peace to limit the number of licences issued, by apportioning them to the population of each place, and by granting them to persons of a respectable character, a multitude of grievances would be redressed, to which the innocent spouse, and the helpless infant are daily exposed.'

Another vicar, the Reverend Colin Mackenzie of Stornoway on the Isle of Lewis also wrote for the *Statistical Account*. He was equally unsympathetic, confirming the reputation men of the cloth as anti-alcohol, whatever the circumstances: 'It is a curious circumstance, that, time out of rememberance, their maidservants were in the habit of drinking, every morning, a wine glass full of whisky, which their mistress gave them; this barbarous custom became so well established by length of time, that if the practice of it should happen to be neglected or forgotten in a family, even once, discontent and idleness throughout the day, on the part of the maid or maids, would be the sure consequence. However, since the stoppage of the distilleries took place, the people of the town found it necessary to unite in the resolution of abolishing the practice, by withholding the dear cordial from their female domestics, but not without the precaution of making a compensation to them in money for their grievous loss; and it is said, that even this is not satisfactory, and that, in some families, the dram is still given privately, to preserve peace and good order.'

Number of gallons of whisky sold to just one man by the Springbank Distillery of Campbeltown, western Scotland, in 1828, its inaugural year.

One for the road!
(But what's he got in the knotted handkerchief?)

THE HARD STUFF

What is a single malt whisky?
Answer on page 153.

SHOME MISHTAKE SHURELY?

For the first time in more than a century, the tax on Scotch whisky was reduced in 1995.

INGREDIENTS FOR SUCCESS

Summer Scotch

1 dram of Scotch
3 dashes of Crème de Menthe
1 lump of ice
Fill glass to the brim with soda.

QUOTE UNQUOTE

I'm on a whisky diet. I've lost three days already!
Tommy Cooper, British comedian

MAD WINDHAM

Anyone travelling on Britain's Eastern Counties Railway in the early 1860s might have been surprised to come across a railwayman with a difference. On different days this absurdly well-spoken railwayman with the aristocratic demeanour and rather haughty air would appear as a porter, a driver or a fireman. What was even more remarkable about him was that he worked for no pay. The railwayman in question was William Frederick Windham, or Whisky Mad Windham as he became known.

Windham was born in 1840, and heir to ancient Felbrigg Hall in Norfolk, in the east of England, and all its estates. He was worth a fortune but by the end of his short life he'd squandered or given all of it away. He once said that the only time he was truly happy was when he had a glass of whisky in his hand or was on the footplate of a locomotive engine. Certainly Windham hated his aristocratic upbringing and, kept from the things he really wanted to do, he grew ever more eccentric.

He obtained a guard's uniform, with belt, pouch and whistle; and in this guise he became a familiar figure on the Eastern Counties Railway. On one occasion – unquestionably the railway journey he enjoyed most – he was driver in the morning, guard in the afternoon and whisky-drinking porter in the evening.

When Windham got married, his wife immediately persuaded him to sign all his money and property over to her. She then threw him out of the family home and he rented a room in a coaching inn in Norwich where he spent his days permanently dressed as a railway guard and holding whisky parties for fellow railway enthusiasts. He died in 1866, whisky glass in hand and still in his railway guard's uniform.

FOR 'JOHN BARLEYCORN' READ 'WHISKY'

And they hae taen his very heart's blood,
And drank it round and round;
And still the more and more they drank,
Their joy did more abound.
John Barleycorn was a hero bold,
Of noble enterprise,
For if you do but taste his blood,
'Twill make your courage rise.

Robbie Burns, *John Barleycorn*

THE HARD STUFF

When did blending first appear?
Answer on page 153.

SECOND-HAND USAGE

Distillers use the following for maturing whisky:
Bourbon barrels of American oak
English oak sherry butts from the Bodegas of Spain
Port pipes from Portugal

WHISKY IN FILM

The Moonshine War, **1970**
Adapted by Elmore Leonard from his own novel, it is an amiable caper about whisky hijacking in hillbilly country.

North Sea Hijack, **1980**
Roger Moore plays an anti-terrorist expert who enjoys sewing, raising cats – and drinking whisky at 10am.

Local Hero, **1983**
Peter Riegert plays Mac, a young executive sent to negotiate setting up an oil refinery in a Scottish fishing village. He enjoys the food and the whisky so much that things don't go exactly as planned.

Withnail & I, **1987**
Withnail (Richard E Grant) and I (Paul McGann) blow Monty's (Richard Griffiths) money for Wellington boots on quadruple whiskies.

Dukes of Hazzard, **2005**
For four generations the Duke family has been engaged in illegal whisky making.

What do you mean, you've never before made seared Glenmorangie Whisky and citrus marinated loin of roe deer with beetroot dauphinoise, wilted spinach and grand veneur sauce? Better start now, then. This recipe serves six.

Beetroot dauphinoise
8 Maris Piper potatoes
4 fresh beetroot, cooked
1 pint double cream
1 clove garlic
1 onion, chopped
Seasoning to taste

Sweat the garlic and chopped onion in butter and cream, reduce by ⅓. Then slice a thin layer of potatoes in a greaseproof tray followed by a thin layer of passed cream. Next, place a layer of sliced beetroot in the tray until it is full. Bake on gas mark 5 for at least 40 minutes until set.

Grand veneur sauce
Sweat 4 finely chopped shallots in butter. Add 4 tablespoons of white wine vinegar, reduce by half. Add crushed black peppercorns to taste, half a pint of game/veal sauce. Finish with a touch of double cream and pass through a sieve.

Marinade for venison (4 to 6 hours)
Only marinade for 4 to 6 hours otherwise it will become too strong.
2 oranges and 2 lemons, squeezed
6 sprigs thyme
4 garlic cloves
1 onion, 1 carrot, 1 celery stick, chopped
6 x 7oz pieces loins
1 double measure of Glenmorangie Ten Years Old

Wash and pick two packets of spinach. Pat dry marinated roe deer or venison, heat a sauté pan with a little oil until it's almost smoking, seal off the deer quickly and season. Place in a hot oven, gas mark 5 for 10 minutes approximately, remove and rest for 5 minutes in a warm place.

Gather all accompaniments and place meat in the oven for a further 10 minutes until medium rare – the cooking time depends on the thickness of the meat and your preferred degree of cooking. (The meat should always be rested.) Meanwhile sweat the spinach in butter, season and drain. Garnish with season vegetables. Savour and enjoy.

Recipe courtesy of David Graham, Head Chef at
Glenmorangie House, Cadboll, Tain, Ross-shire, Scotland

GLASS IMAGES

Whisky glasses have been decorated with:

Pictures of Marilyn Monroe
Real insects trapped in bubbles in the glass
The devil
Former US presidents
Hollywood stars
Famous murderers

SINGING WHISKY'S PRAISES:
FOUR SONG TITLES

He Sold her for a Dram
Nell Gow's Farewell to Whisky
How I Miss a Sup or Twae
The Ballad of the Blue Brewery

DECLINE AND FALL

In 1780 there were 1,228 distilleries in Ireland. By 1823 that number had fallen to just 40.

MEDICINE MEN

Right across the world and usually well away from its Scottish and Irish homelands, whisky has come to be used in a number of traditional medicines.

Appalachian Indians use whisky mixed with rhubarb as a cure for arthritis, or mixed with rattlesnake root, ginseng, wild cherry and goldenseal for a cure for rheumatism.

In the early 1800s, the Pennsylvania Dutch in rural America used a dubious mixture of whisky and tobacco to cure their children's colic.

Meanwhile, Yaa Dong is a traditional Thai medicinal tonic, made by steeping herbs, barks, stalks and shoots in whisky. Used as a remedy for fatigue, circulatory problems, poor appetite and sexual dysfunction, the many variations on the recipe are said to originate from the temples where some believe it was developed by monks as a justification for drinking whisky.

*Drinking whisky is a sure way to convince
yourself you can sing!*

LOST AT SEA

Underwater archaeologists reckon that more than 60,000 bottles of whisky lie unbroken and unspoiled beneath the surface of the world's oceans. Many ships were lost in the nineteenth century – and thousands would have had whisky aboard. The whisky is likely to be well corked and still as good today as when it went down, yet the cost of retrieving even a fraction of it makes it likely that the lost whisky will stay at the bottom of the sea for a very long time, despite its increasing value.

Pennsylvania, like so much of America, was a troubled place at the end of the eighteenth century. The US had only recently declared its independence from Britain and in Pennsylvania settlers still fought with the North-American Indians who resented their land being taken from them. Then there was the difficulty of the central government persuading individual states that they could not always do just as they pleased – this was a particular problem in Pennsylvania where remote communities carried on as they always had.

But what was seen as the 'Indian problem' increased until it was decided that a tax would be levied to pay for the army needed to defeat the native peoples – and what could they tax that was sure to raise a great deal of money? The answer was whiskey.

The whiskey tax was reckoned to produce more than 20 million dollars – enough to pay for an almost endless series of attacks on the Indians. A tax of seven cents a gallon was eventually imposed. The whiskey tax had some odd consequences. Whiskey sold in one direction – in Washington County – sold for about 25 cents a gallon. Selling whiskey on the other, eastern side of the mountains brought in about 50 cents a gallon. Because the tax was imposed where the whiskey was made instead of where it was sold, the western whiskey tax was about 28% while the eastern whiskey had a 14% tax. Those who made whiskey for their own consumption also had to pay tax. Resentment was huge as whiskey trials were held in Philadelphia rather than in local courts, and the travel and inconvenience also fuelled discontent.

By 1791 the whiskey tax was being resisted in many places. A full-scale whiskey insurrection began – whiskey-makers refused to pay the tax, and to attend court, and those who tried to enforce the law were sometimes tarred and feathered.

Eventually blood was shed at General Neville's house when the local militia tried to arrest Neville. His men opened fire and the militia retreated. But then they attacked Neville's home, burning the house and barns, although the inhabitants escaped. There were many other bloody skirmishes until 7 August 1794, when George Washington began mobilising nearly 13,000 troops. He offered an amnesty to the insurrectionists but required that they accept the whiskey tax.

Washington's army began rounding up suspects who were marched to Philadelphia to stand trial. Many leaders escaped but the whiskey rebellion was largely over. The rebellion had failed, but it did publicise the plight of the settlers and helped the new American state understand that dissent must be allowed at a regional level. It was, if you like, whiskey's contribution to the history and development of democracy.

FAMOUS FISHING FLIES

Whisky and orange

Whisky flash

Whisky mac

Whisky nymph

INFAMOUS PEOPLE WHO LOVED WHISKY

Al Capone (American gangster)

Dr Crippen (American-born British murderer)

Queen Elizabeth I of England

Earl Haig (commander of British forces in World War I)

Lord Lucan (missing British aristocrat, alleged murderer)

Mussolini (Italian statesman)

Pol Pot (leader of Cambodian Khmer Rouge guerrillas)

Tsar Peter the Great of Russia

Sir Walter Raleigh (English explorer)

THE WHITE LADY

Every distillery has its ghosts. The old buildings echo with mysterious creaks and groans that quicken the pulse of even the most cynical observer. Naturally, the home of Scotland's favourite malt wouldn't be complete without its own resident ghost.

Indeed, legend has it that the Glenmorangie's Men of Tain have been frequently distracted from the creation of one spirit by the presence of another: the White Lady. She's been known to flit through the Distillery in the wee small hours weeping and wailing, terrifying anyone she meets on the way.

Though her legend has been passed down from generation to generation, she's been noted by her absence in recent times. Distillery Manager, Graham Eunson, offers a simple explanation for her reticence: 'Ah yes, the White Lady,' he sighs. 'Well I think the truth is that she was a figment of a fertile imagination, though I know that the whole story has very practical roots.' It does indeed. In the old days when Glenmorangie had its floor maltings at the distillery, the malt had to be shovelled around the clock. One sleepy shoveller could ruin the next day's mash by falling asleep at his post. The presence of the White Lady (or at least the threat of an imminent apparition) was enough to keep the nightshift on their toes. 'Whether she ever existed or not is highly debatable,' admits Graham, 'the only spirits around here,' he adds, 'are the ones that we make!'

WHISKY FOR MUMMY

There is substantial evidence that the elaborate procedures involved in the process of ancient Egyptian mummification involved the use of a distilled grain spirit that would not have been entirely unlike modern whisky.

We know that the Egyptians used fermented grain to produce a highly intoxicating brew and many of the graves that were opened up in the first great wave of archaeological interest in the nineteenth century show signs of a liquor having been poured over the dead almost as the last ritual before their coffins were closed for ever. The processes and chemicals used by the ancient Egyptians to embalm their dead are still not entirely understood, but they were highly sophisticated and extremely effective, which is why so many mummies have come down to us in such a wonderful state of preservation.

Ironically, the damage to many mummies was caused by pouring that last pitcher of what may well have been a whisky-like drink over the torso of the deceased; being liquid it caused the sort of decay that the rest of the embalming processes were designed to prevent. Major damage to the most famous mummy of all – Tutankhamen – was almost certainly caused in this way. One only hopes that as well as having it poured over him in death he managed to drink plenty while he was still alive!

QUOTE UNQUOTE

What whiskey will not cure, there is no cure for.
Irish proverb

DRAM-ATIC WRITING

Duncan Dhu made haste to bring out the pair of pipes that was his principal possession, and to set before his guests a mutton-ham and a bottle of that drink which they call Athole brose, and which is made of old whiskey, strained honey and sweet cream, slowly beaten together in the right order and proportion. The two enemies were still on the very breach of a quarrel; but down they sat, one upon each side of the peat fire, with a mighty show of politeness. Maclaren pressed them to taste his mutton-ham and 'the wife's brose,' reminding them the wife was out of Athole and had a name far and wide for her skill in that confection. But Robin put aside these hospitalities as bad for the breath.

Robert Louis Stevenson, *Kidnapped*

DEATH OF A POET

As is well known, Welsh poet Dylan Thomas was fond of a drink of whisky. In fact he became hugely dependent on alcohol and died at the age of 39, with drink-related problems contributing to his early demise. He first developed a taste for alcohol while working in journalism and eventually grew to revel in the romantic image of the drunken poet. Alcohol became part of his home life with both he and his wife Caitlin being drunk on their wedding day. Dylan had a wide reputation for being a drunk, and while he tended to exaggerate his excesses, he definitely had a penchant for the hard stuff. The story of his death shows this more than anything. On what was to be his final trip he arrived in New York in October 1953, already referring to Caitlin as 'my widow'.

He drank heavily while he was in the Big Apple and after a particularly big night out uttered the now legendary phrase: 'I've had 18 straight whiskies. I think that's the record.' They weren't his last words though and he awoke the next day, not unsurprisingly, feeling ill. He spent the next few days flitting between bars and being attended by a doctor before finally being taken to hospital in a coma. Caitlin arrived from Wales reportedly asking 'is the bloody man dead yet?' Thomas finally died on 9 November and the post-mortem revealed that he had died of pneumonia, with pressure on the brain and a fatty liver given as contributing factors. He left behind no will but a body of work that included the poem 'Do Not Go Gentle Into That Good Night' and the radio play *Under Milk Wood*. Many have called him one of the greatest poets of the twentieth century, and he will always be remembered as closely associated with alcohol, and whisky in particular.

DRAM-ATIC WRITING

Sir, Damn thee and God Damn thy two Purblind Eyes thou Buger and thou Death looking Son of a Bitch O that I had bin there (with my company) for they sake when thou tookes them men of Mine on Board the Speedwell Cutter on Monday ye 14 Decr. I would drove thee and all they Gang to Hell wher thou belongest thou Devil Incarnet Go Down thou Hell Hound into thy Kennell below & Bathe thy Self in that Sulpherous Lake that has bin so long Prepared for such as thee for it is time the World was rid of such a Monster thou art no Man but a Devil thou fiend I hope thou will soon fall into Hell like a star from the Sky; there to lie (unpitied) & unrelented of any for Ever and Ever Which God Grant of his Infinite Mercy Amen.

Letter from J Spurier, Whisky Smuggler;
Fordingbridge, January 1700

BEST SELLING

Quick stats about whisky sales

- About 10% of Scottish agriculture, and one in 50 of Scottish jobs rely on the Scotch whisky industry.

- Glenmorangie is Scotland's favourite malt

- Ballantine's is considered to be one of the oldest and also one of the most expensive blends available.

QUOTE UNQUOTE

Whisky – God's apology.
Anon

UNDER THE SPELL OF CADBOLL CASTLE

Visitors to Glenmorangie House at Cadboll, near Tain, will immediately notice that adjacent to the shining whitewashed walls of this five-star country house is a considerably older building that now lies in ruins. Cadboll Castle – a listed ancient monument – is now protected by Historic Scotland.

The castle dates back to the mid sixteenth century and has a long and chequered history. Curiously, according to legend, nobody has ever died within the walls of Cadboll Castle. In 1878, the editor of the *Celtic Magazine*, Alexander Mackenzie, published a collection of popular Highland stories under the title 'The Tales and Legends of the Highlands'. One of the selected tales was 'The Spell of Cadboll'.

Mackenzie's romantic spirit was obviously captivated by the plight of the tragic Lady May Macleod, who mourned the death of her betrothed for more than 50 years, as a recluse within Cadboll Castle before 'disease laid hold of her limbs, paralysed, unable to move, she would fain have died, but the spell of Cadboll was upon her, death could not enter its walls'.

QUOTE UNQUOTE

Mary Kate Danaher: Could you use a little water in your whiskey?
Michaleen Flynn: When I drink whiskey, I drink whiskey and when I drink water, I drink water.
From the film *The Quiet Man* (1952)

*When whisky came corked, the forgetful had to adopt other,
more extreme methods to get at their favourite tipple!*

HAIR TODAY

A long-running debate in an old *Daily Mirror* regular column called
the 'Old Codgers' concerned likely cures for hair loss. During the
1960s when the column was at the height of its popularity it was
filled several times a week with suggested cures sent in by readers –
many claimed that their secret recipe had been handed down in the
family or was a secret from a long-vanished monastery.

Among the more bizarre cures was burnt toast rubbed into the
afflicted area; a rubber bathing cap coated on the inside with a mix
of water, sugar and milk of magnesia; and best of all, lint bandages
soaked in whisky and strapped to the head. The wearer was
supposed to go to bed with the whisky bandages each night for a
week – history does not record if the system ever worked.

Irish whiskey was once the dominant brand in world whiskey production – in fact the Scottish are recorded in the latter half of the nineteenth century as having exported their whisky mixed with a drop of the Irish. But after Ireland became a republic in 1926 the new state taxed whiskey heavily and fell out badly with the British government. This became something of an economic war and a policy of protectionism and worsening relations with England destroyed the UK market for Irish whiskey during World War II. The already precarious situation was made even worse when the Irish government capped their whiskey exports. The gap created by this folly was quickly filled by the Scots, who had also done well during Prohibition in America. Irish whiskey had been hugely popular in nineteenth-century America and when Prohibition came bootleggers sold as Irish whiskey some terrible concoctions which severely damaged the reputation of Irish whiskey. The Scots were able to get ahead at this time because they shipped their whisky to British outposts, like the Bahamas, from which it was an easy run into America. The Scots whisky was good, so as Irish whiskey lost its reputation, Scottish whisky gained a reputation it has never lost.

With the end of Prohibition no one wanted Irish whiskey – they wanted the wonderful stuff they'd enjoyed illicitly for 13 long years. Ironically it was an Irishman who knocked another nail in the coffin of Irish whiskey – Irish customs officer, Aeneas Coffey had watched the traditional pot still whiskey process that produced the full-bodied flavour typical of Irish whiskey but he invented a more efficient method for continuous distillation in 1830. Irish distillers thought the Coffey still was awful – it produced what they referred to as a 'silent spirit' – a tasteless substance compared to whiskey produced in the traditional pot still.

Scottish distillers loved the new invention on the other hand, but this caused a dilemma: which was whisky – was it the pot still spirit or the Coffey spirit? In 1905 a famous legal case in London tried to decide. On the one side were Irish advocates of the pot still and on the other Scottish advocates of the Coffey apparatus. The judge ruled that pot still whisky was the only true whiskey. Whisky made from spirit distilled in Coffey Stills could no longer be called whisky.

Then in 1908 a Royal Commission, possibly biased against the Irish who were agitating for Home Rule, reversed the decision: they found themselves 'unable to recommend that the use of the word whiskey should be restricted to spirit manufactured by the pot still process.' Coffey Still Whisky was cheaper to produce than pot still whiskey and once again the Irish product – still considered by many to be the superior tipple – lost out to the Hibernian's favourite tipple.

INGREDIENTS FOR SUCCESS

Green Mist

1 dram of Scotch
1 dash of Crème de Menthe
Juice of half a lemon

Mix the ingredients, strain into a glass. Decorate with a sprig of mint.

WIT AND WHISKY

– Doctor I have a drinking problem!
– What is it?
– When I'm drinking whisky I have two hands but only one mouth.

DRAM-ATIC WRITING

Having long been possessed with an ardent desire to see the Distilleries of Scotland and Ireland, I took the first opportunity that presented itself, and, knowing the task set before me would occupy at least two years, made arrangements to transfer my duties to others. It was at first thought desirable that my tour should commence at the Orkneys; but, the weather proving unfavourable, my plan of entering the land of Whisky by the sea was abandoned in favour of the iron road to Glasgow. We – for I was not doomed to travel alone – started from Euston by the night mail, having previously invested in a copy of 'Morewood' and one or two other hooks on Distillation to study on our journey. Nothing of note occurred on the journey, except that we got a little amusement out of our fellow travellers – one of them a gentleman in clerical attire, catching some fragments of our conversation on spirits, evidently mistook us for important officers in the Salvation Army. Seeing this we puzzled him, and in answer to his enquiries, informed him that we had just started on a long and tedious pilgrimage to the spirit land, and that ours was a mission of investigation into the creation, development and perfection of crude spirits into 'spirits made perfect.' One of our party here produced his flask and explained to our reverend friend what kind of missionaries we were, when, to our surprise, after taking a 'wee drappie,' and like Oliver Twist, asking for more, the pious-looking brother offered to join us in our excursions, that he might do the tasting, and we the writing. This generous offer we declined.

Alfred Barnard,
The Whisky Distilleries of the United Kingdom, 1887

DOWN ON THE FARM

In George Orwell's dark satire on totalitarianism, *Animal Farm*, pigs take over a farmhouse and start to discover the various pleasures and pitfalls of human dominance. One of these dubious pleasures is drinking whisky. The pigs, led by Napoleon, find a barrel of whisky in the cellar and go about drinking the whole thing. A drunken night ensues, followed by a rather large hangover. So large in fact that the pigs believe Napoleon is dying. But as the effects wear off the pigs start to look more fondly on whisky and even buy booklets about distilling and buy barley to sow. Orwell was making a statement about the disruptive and addictive nature of alcohol on man, but to a whisky lover it could just be construed that even pigs are whisky fans!

FAMOUS FACES

People who have appeared on the front cover
of UK-based *Whisky Magazine:*

Humphrey Bogart
Pierce Brosnan
Sean Connery
Billy Connolly
Madonna
Bill Murray
Michael Palin
Prince Charles
Jackie Stewart

PROFIT DILUTION

During Prohibition in America whiskey was adulterated in many ways. At first a little water was added – just 10% water meant the whiskey went a lot further and profits which were already high for the mafia gangs and others really began to soar. Some clubs and speakeasies then realised that such was the desperation of their customers for whiskey that they were usually drunk within the first hour after they'd arrived – this meant that staff were instructed to gradually serve increasingly watered down spirits but at the price they would have charged for the first few drinks. It is said that mafia profits were so vast during this period that whatever setbacks from law enforcement agencies they might later suffer they had enough financial reserves to keep them going for more than a century.

ENOUGH TO GO ROUND

The word 'galore' – as in *Whisky Galore!* – comes from the Gaelic 'gu leòir', meaning 'plenty'.

A WHISKY-DRINKING JUDGE

For those of us who are not French speakers, the phrase '*porter ce vieux whisky au juge blond qui fume*' might need some explanation. It definitely includes whisky, but why? Well, translated, it roughly means 'take this old whisky to the fair-haired judge who is smoking.' A strange piece of advice you may think, but there is method behind the madness. The phase is the shortest pangram in the French language, a pangram being a sentence that uses all the letters of the alphabet. The best known one in English is 'the quick brown fox jumps over the lazy dog'.

QUOTE UNQUOTE

If there's room...
Scottish poet George Mackay Brown, when given
a whisky and asked if he'd like water with it

WHISKY MAKES YOU FRISKY

Sunset Boulevard in Los Angeles is one of the most famous roads in the world, in no small part thanks to the 1950 film *Sunset Boulevard* directed by Billy Wilder. These days, the street is known as a party venue, especially the mile and a half stretch between Hollywood and Beverly Hills that has been dubbed the 'Sunset Strip'. This part of town boasts dozens of bars, including the Whisky Bar. Apparently a favourite among rock stars it has seen the likes of U2, Jeff Beck, Rod Stewart and Nirvana darken its doorways over the years. The bar, realising its popularity with rockers, built a recording studio nearby where musicians can lay down some new tracks before piping the results directly over the sound system in the bar while relaxing with a wee dram.

It's not all sweetness and light though, as the Whisky Bar was the scene of a superstar bust-up between actors Don Johnson (of *Miami Vice* fame) and perennial British baddie Gary Oldman. Johnson offered a drink to Oldman, which he refused and the two apparently got into an insult and shoving match, which had to be broken up by none other than *The Godfather* actor James Caan. Only in LA!

THE HARD STUFF

Can you sell two-year-old whisky?
Answer on page 153.

TRANSPORTING

One of Scotland's smaller whisky distillers, in the days before whisky distillers were all licensed, noticed that a railway line had been built not far from the bothy where he conducted his illicit activities. The distiller – who had grown quite wealthy on the proceeds of his whisky making – decided that the slow business of transporting his wares by packhorse should cease and knowing almost nothing about the new railway and the way it worked, thought he would simply make use of the new iron rails. He had a carriage made with iron flanged wheels and found that two ponies could pull the cart with half a tonne of whisky in it. He came unstuck when the cart was greeted by an iron steam engine travelling at 15 miles per hour in the opposite direction. The poor ponies were killed, the whisky spilled and the cart smashed. The distiller, who survived, was arrested.

SACRE BLEU!

The French drink more whisky in a week than cognac in a month.

PITY TO WASTE IT

Most whisky aficionados would consider the mixing of very old malt whisky, in this case, Ardbeg, with anything other than water to be a mortal sin. However, as the men who make Ardbeg are indeed, mere mortals, mistakes can happen.

At Ardbeg in 2003, the wrong lever was pulled at the wrong time and a substantial (and financially significant) amount of very, very old Ardbeg was mixed with a small amount of 12-year-old Glen Moray, another of Glenmorangie's malts. Like many a sin before it, the result of this union was the birth of something somewhat unexpected, but nevertheless very welcome, being a superb blended malt whisky. A serendipitous outcome indeed, which is why it was promptly bottled and named Serendipity – 'for 'twas a "pity" to waste it...' – and what might have been money down the drain became a liquid asset!

DOING IT FOR THE KIDS

During the 2003 events for Britain's Children in Need yearly charity drive, one of the ways money was raised was through an auction of gifts donated by top politicians. Gifts included a bottle of House of Commons red wine donated by Tony Blair, and a bottle of port from Conservative leader Michael Howard. Scottish Charles Kennedy, leader of the Liberal Democrats donated a bottle of whisky. It was for charity, but why would anyone want to give away a bottle of whisky?

THE WITCH WHO LOVED WHISKY

Alfred Barnard's The Whisky Distilleries of the United Kingdom *includes the following fascinating account of Scotland's last witch:*

The next afternoon we left Ardrishaig behind us and embarked on board the 'Linnet', as pretty and comfortable a boat as sails on any canal in the kingdom. We steamed through the Crinan Canal, on which there are fifteen locks, and a delightful time we had. There were four of us, and how we all revelled in the glory of that summer day's procession; now we would alight from the boat and walk into the woods, or basten forward and refresh ourselves with milk and wild strawberries, vended on the canal banks, or return to the boat to the next lock and smoke a cigar. It was quite easy to keep pace with the steamer, and most of our fellow passengers exercised themselves in this way. After leaving the locks, the canal winds round the beautiful wooded ridge of Knapdale, and we are in the land of spells and witchcraft. Here, thirty-four years ago, the last known witch was burned.

Start not, gentle reader, it was neither by the law nor Judge Lynch she suffered. She was a masculine kind of old woman... Sarah of the bog, as she was called, was extensively engaged in smuggling, and unlike Meg Merrilies, she had not borne twelve 'buirdly sans and daughters', but had lived like Queen Bess 'in maiden meditation fancy free'. Ta cover up her illicit traffic, she practised necromancy, and the inhabitants of the district being very superstitious, propitiated her good graces by providing peats, potatoes, and meal, and many instances of the belief in her powers and the manner in which she levied her contributions were related to us. But Sarah grew old, and having acquired the taste for stimulants amid the exciting scenes of her youth, like Neil Gow, she 'Dearly Lo'ed the whisky, oh', and regularly dosed herself with the contents of her whisky keg. One night she drank too much, stumbled and fell into the fire, and when the house was next visited, the miserable creature was found with her head black and burned to a cinder.

SMALL CONSOLATION

A Canadian whisky miniature collector managed to gather together more than three thousand miniature whisky bottles in what is believed to be a world record collection – his haul included rare whiskies from all over the world together with tiny bottles of the cheapest whiskies from as far afield as Ireland and Taiwan.

He is reported to have been distraught when the collection – every last bottle – was stolen and never recovered. He decided to start the collection all over again having received a generous payout from his insurers, but this time he announced that he would be drinking the contents of each bottle first!

WHISKY IN FILM

Whisky Galore! 1949
When a Scottish island falls prey to a whisky shortage, the islanders are desolate. But when by chance a ship is sunk with a cargo of 50,000 cases of whisky, they see their salvation.

The African Queen, 1951
During filming John Huston and Humphrey Bogart drank only whisky, while Katharine Hepburn and the crew drank only water. As a result, she and the rest of the crew suffered severe bouts of dysentery, but Huston and Bogart remained unscathed.

Lost in Translation, 2003
The inspiration for having Bob Harris (played by Bill Murray) do a Suntory Whisky commercial was partially inspired by the fact that Sofia Coppola's father, Francis Ford Coppola, made a real Suntory commercial with Akira Kurosawa in the 1970s.

OLD SOAKS

Whisky has long been used by ramblers, soldiers and others prone to blisters. Theories of exactly how to use the amber nectar to guard against becoming footsore vary – one source reckons that for years in Scotland shepherds would soak a new pair of boots in water mixed with a little whisky. In more recent times ramblers would soak their feet in a basin of pure whisky for a few hours before setting out on a long journey. Vinegar for the same purpose became fashionable in the 1970s yet there is no evidence at all that soaking the feet in anything actually works!

AN EXTRAORDINARY ESCAPE

Many hair's breadth escapes from almost certain death have been recorded in the annals of railway history, one of the most wonderful being that of the man who, in the early days of corridor trains, stepped out on the wrong side of a Great Western express running at 60 miles per hour, and alighted on the tracks without receiving a scratch.

When asked how on earth he managed to step out of a high-speed train by mistake he explained that he'd been enjoying a glass or two of whisky with a few friends in the buffet carriage when, as was his habit at home, he decided to get some fresh air! He insisted to a local newspaper reporter that if he'd been drinking an effete beverage – like wine – he would certainly have been killed.

BIRDS THAT ARE REPUTED TO HAVE DRUNK WHISKY

Budgerigars
Choughs
Parrots
Red kites
Sparrows

THE WONDER OF WOOD

From Tain in Scotland to Missouri – the journey to discover the best wood to mature its spirit in has been a long one for Glenmorangie. Their research, which started in the 1980s, led them to the slow-growth wood found in certain parts of the Ozark Mountains in the US.

Growing on the shaded side of the mountain, this 100-year-old slow-growing oak results in very porous wood, meaning it is ideal for whisky maturation. Once the trees are felled they are air-dried or seasoned for a couple of years to maintain their open texture. The wood is crafted into casks and their journey to Tain in Scotland continues via Kentucky where they are used to mature bourbon. This seasons the wood by absorbing any harsh or undesirable elements.

Finally, the ex-bourbon casks are shipped to Tain, filled with Glenmorangie spirit and left to mature in the distillery's traditional low-ceilinged, earthen-floored warehouses – a gentle end to a long journey.

Littlemill Glasgow, in 1880. The Distillery is a very old work, having been built about the year 1800, but considerably improved and enlarged by the late Mr. Hay in 1875 to meet the increased demand for his product. The Whisky is Malt only, and the peat used in drying is brought from Stornaway and Perthshire; the water comes from a shady glen away up in the Kilpatrick Hills, and is brought down to a reservoir close by.

There are four Duty free Warehouses holding 6,500 casks and there is a compact little cooperage employing two men all the year round. The Whisky is sent to England, Ireland, India and the Colonies. The Firm bas a Warehouse at 36, Douglas Street, Glasgow, where they blend, rack, and bottle for home use and exportation. The annual output is 150,000 gallons.

Alfred Barnard, *The Whisky Distilleries of the United Kingdom*, 1887

QUOTE UNQUOTE

The light music of whiskey falling into a glass – an agreeable interlude.
James Joyce, writer

WHEN IS A BOURBON NOT A BOURBON?

When it's Jack Daniel's. Actually, this also applies to the George Dickel brand.

Whisky connoisseurs are very method-specific when it comes to their choice refreshment, and in the case of Jack and George, there is a crucial intervention that sets them apart from bourbon – even though up to that point they are, to all intents and purposes, eligible for the club.

The disputed intervention is the Lincoln County Process, which involves dripping the liquor as slowly as possible through charcoal in order to filter out impurities. Trouble is, in the eyes, or rather taste buds, of the whisky boffins, Lincoln County replaces what it removes – and true bourbon must not be given any form of flavour-enhancement. As it's forged from sugar maple, the charcoal used in the filtering gives back a sweetness that, according to house rules, puts the treated fluid in a different class.

Consequently, Jack and George both have to live with the more prosaic title of Tennessee Whiskey – but what the heck? Bourbons are 10 a penny... and Jack and George are the kings of their category.

Scotch Tom Collins

1 dram of Scotch
6 dashes of lemon juice
Ice
Fill a tall glass to the brim with soda.

OH, BROTHER

Like most sports, fishing has its share of tall tales – many concerning whisky, which seems to go with fishing as a horse goes with a carriage. Such as the following:

A fisherman who made his living by catching and selling salmon from a remote Scottish river frequently went for months at a time without seeing or speaking to another human being, but he had lived in his isolated bothy for many years perfectly happily.

The old man had two brothers who were even older than he was – one probably in his late seventies, the other almost certainly more than 80. Then, one terrible winter, the eldest brother died. It was too cold to take him to the nearest town so his brothers packed him in ice and waited for the spring.

When the weather improved they took their dead brother on a deer pony to the nearest railway station. The brothers sat their dead – and very well-preserved brother – propped up between them and they laid out three glasses of whisky on the table.

Certain that the next stop – half an hour away – was theirs they went off to buy more whisky in the buffet car, but while they were there the train stopped at a small station and a man struggled aboard with a very heavy suitcase. He dragged it into the first compartment he could find which happened to be where the dead brother sat leaning and apparently fast asleep in the corner.

Just as he'd managed almost to heft his suitcase onto the luggage rack he lost his grip and it crashed down on to the 'sleeping' passenger spilling his whisky and knocking him to the floor. Horrified, the traveller lifted his suitcase off the elderly man but immediately realised the old man was dead. The traveller was horror-struck. He panicked and decided there was just one thing to do: he dragged the old man to the door, opened it and pushed him out into the snowy darkness.

Two minutes later the traveller was back in the compartment trying to compose himself when the two brothers returned from the buffet car with a fresh supply of whisky.

'Where on earth is our brother?' they asked.

'Oh him,' came the reply, 'he got off at the last stop.'

Uncle Sam's generosity didn't extend to free whisky!

THE HARD STUFF

What is considered the optimum age for whisky?
Answer on page 153.

CHURCH-GOING, GOING, GONE

Anglican vicars were traditionally always enthusiastic whisky drinkers and in earlier times they could be very uncooperative if their supplies dried up or if their bishops objected to their drinking. An eighteenth-century Shropshire vicar who was told that he must drink less before taking the service on a Sunday is a case in point. He was so outraged that he made wooden cut-out versions of half a dozen of his parishioners (after discovering that their complaints had led to the bishop's injunction), propped them up in the pews and locked the church doors. For months he refused to allow his parishioners into the church on a Sunday but he continued to drink his whisky and then preach to the assembled wooden figures. It was only when the bishop threatened to oust him from his living that the vicar relented – but he never gave up his whisky drinking and the bishop never mentioned it again.

DRAM-ATIC WRITING

On Thursday, January 11, 1816 between 7pm-8pm, two customs officials intercepted at Townhead Toll four burly ruffians safeguarding the transit of a single bladder of spirits. This they not only refused to give up, but the bearer, with heavy bludgeon raised, rushed on one of the excisemen and fiercely assailed him. The latter being very strong, seized his opponent and managed to drag him to the Bell o' the Brae, while the other gauger with drawn cutlass, kept at bay the other smugglers, though the rapidly gathering and none too friendly crowd greatly impeded their movements. Repeatedly the leading smuggler grasped the blade of the officer's cutlass and the efforts to release this weapon, his hands became horribly gashed. By and by a police patrol came tardily on the scene and with their help the prisoner was conveyed to a point opposite the gales of the old college. Here his friends closed up to support him and made an onslaught so irresistible that in the end the constables fled for their lives and the smugglers got clear away. Next morning the excisemen learned, to their chagrin, that all this uproar and commotion, all the direful din and confusion at the Bell o' the Brae, had been raised as a blind to conceal the safe running of a huge load of whisky elsewhere.

Weekly Scotsman,
9 October 1909

QUOTE UNQUOTE

A good gulp of hot whiskey at bedtime –
it's not very scientific, but it helps.
Alexander Fleming, recommending treatment for the common cold

SPIRITED AWAY

In the 1830s when the railway was still young and thrilling, neither the public nor the specialists were convinced that the right system – that is steam – had been hit upon.

The fact that motive power that did not involve the horse had been discovered seems to have inspired all kinds of ideas for new fangled and often outlandish modes of transport. One reputable scientist suggested an 'entirely new system of railway carriage, which may be propelled without the aid of steam at an extraordinary speed, exceeding 60 miles an hour using distilled whisky as the combustible fuel...' No details were given and history does not record if the engine ever got beyond the drawing board.

DRAMBRUCIE

It is said that the hugely successful tactical guerrilla warfare techniques adopted by Robert the Bruce – a Scottish leader who spectacularly defeated the English at the Battle of Bannockburn in 1314 – were fuelled largely by whisky. Hugely potent whisky distilled in the medieval period in Scotland gave Robert the Bruce's men a wild fearlessness that terrified the English. Even today the British army is said to recruit its best soldiers from Scotland.

MAKE UP NEW RULES

When Romania declared war in August 1916, numerous bizarre directives were issued about the dress and behaviour the country's leaders expected of their officers. Uniforms had to be worn in precise ways that dated back to the early nineteenth century; wigs (for certain ceremonial duties) were to be worn at a certain angle, but best of all was the directive which said that only officers above the rank of major were allowed to wear make-up and drink whisky!

A TRADITIONAL IRISH REEL – REEL DRUNK

Early one day the sun wouldn't shine
I was walking down the street not feeling too fine
I saw two old men with a bottle between 'em
And this was the song that I heard them singing

(Chorus) Lord preserve us and protect us,
we've been drinking whiskey 'fore breakfast

Well I stopped by the steps where they was sitting
And I couldn't believe how drunk they were getting
I said 'old men, have you been drinking long?'
They said 'just long enough to be singing this song'

Well they passed me the bottle and I took a little sip
And it felt so good I just couldn't quit
I drank some more and next thing I knew
There were three of us sitting there singing this tune

One by one everybody in town
They heard our ruckus and they all came down
And pretty soon all the streets were ringing
With the sound of the whole town laughing and singing

W IS FOR WHISKY

You can find whisky even in the most sober of military communications, due to its appearance in the NATO phonetic alphabet. The International Civil Aviation Organisation assigned words to the letters of the alphabet so that critical combinations of letters could be pronounced and understood by aircrew speaking over imperfect radio links. Over time the assignment of letters has varied, with early versions of the alphabet being compiled by the RAF and featuring beer for B, monkey for M and nuts for n. In the modern NATO alphabet, whisky is the representative for the letter W and has been used since 1956. But before that whisky was not the W word of choice. Between 1924 and 1956 William was used in all airborne communication.

LIFE SAVER

A famous angling journalist who spent weeks at a time every year fishing for salmon was also a devoted whisky drinker. He had fallen into dozens of Scottish rivers in his time but had always been lucky – either friends were at hand to haul him out or he'd manage to paddle successfully for the shore after the shock of the cold water sobered him up.

But once on the Tweed he very nearly came unstuck. He was fishing wearing a new pair of chest waders and having drunk his usual quantity of whisky he slipped on the gravel and disappeared up to his neck in the fast-flowing water. He was not unduly concerned until he noticed that he could not get the new waders off and they were rapidly filling with water. He began to think this really was the end – he'd thrown away his rod and net but he could feel the gradually increasing weight of water-filled waders pulling him down. He

began to shout and then noticed one of his friends racing along the bank towards him. Next thing the drowning fisherman saw was a large whisky bottle – the sort more commonly seen in pubs and bars – sailing through air towards his head.

The bottle landed with a splash and just out of reach. Then he saw the bottle shooting away back towards the shore and he realised that it had been tied to a length of thick twine. By now he could just keep his head above water and he knew that he had just one more chance – the whisky bottle came sailing through the air and just missed his head. He grabbed it and was slowly pulled to shore. It would be nice to say that he never fished and drank again but it would not be true – he merely arranged for the big empty whisky bottle and its attendant twine to be hung in the fisherman's lodge for future emergencies!

QUOTE UNQUOTE

We borrowed golf from Scotland as we borrowed whiskey. Not because it is Scottish, but because it is good.
Horace G Hutchinson, golfer

CELEBRITIES WHO HAVE ADVERTISED WHISKY

Sean Connery – Suntory Japanese whisky (the same brand Bill Murray promotes in the film *Lost in Translation*)

Sean Connery – Dewar's 12 Special Reserve Scotch whisky

Tommy Cooper – did a voiceover for Bell's Scotch whiskies

Francis Ford Coppola – Suntory Japanese whisky (the film *Lost in Translation* was directed by Sofia Coppola, his daughter, and was based on his experiences of filming ads for Suntory whisky with Akira Kurosawa in the 1970s)

Harry Hill – did a voiceover for Bell's Scotch whiskies

Jools Holland – Bell's Scotch whiskies

Mickey Rourke – Suntory Japanese whisky

DRAM-ATIC WRITING

'Ask my forgiveness!' said Mark, with his accustomed cheerfulness, as he proceeded to unpack the chest. 'The head partner a-asking forgiveness of Co., eh? There must be something wrong in the firm when that happens. I must have the books inspected, and the accounts gone over immediate. Here we are. Everything in its proper place. Here's the salt pork. Here's the biscuit. Here's the whiskey – uncommon good it smells too. Here's the tin pot. This tin pot's a small fortun' in itself! Here's the blankets. Here's the axe. Who says we ain't got a first-rate fit out? I feel as if I was a cadet gone out to Indy, and my noble father was chairman of the Board of Directors. Now, when I've got some water from the stream afore the door and mixed the grog,' cried Mark, running out to suit the action to the word, 'there's a supper ready, comprising every delicacy of the season. Here we are, sir, all complete. For what we are going to receive, et cetrer. Lord bless you, sir, it's very like a gipsy party!'
Charles Dickens, *Martin Chuzzlewit*

AN EXPLOSIVE PROOF –
EQUATION ATTACHED

The 'proof' rating for whisky is a strange subject, mainly because it seems a little bit redundant next to the alcohol percentage – which, let's face it, is what most people are really interested in. Essentially, it is twice the alcohol content as noted by percentage, which means that manufacturers can place a bigger number on their brands' labels and make them look slightly more impressive.

'Proof' was arrived at by trial and error as distillers of three centuries ago attempted to harmonise alcoholic fieriness with the more delicate demands of taste. It wasn't possible to chemically analyse the whisky of the time – save for one, basic method, which had somewhat dangerous implications.

This was to wet a quantity of gunpowder with a sample of the spirit in question, and set it on fire.

If the resulting flame burned yellow, its alcohol content was too high. But the spirit would then be watered down and retested in steady increments until the flame started to burn blue. At this point, the liquor was said to be 'gunpowder proof' – hence the term. A spirit that burned on gunpowder with a perfect, blue flame was given a proof rating of 100, supposedly because the number signifies wholeness and completeness, and was reckoned to contain 50% alcohol to 50% water. Which is why proofs are twice that of percentages: they express an alcohol level of 50% as 100.

A distiller seeking to make his supplies stretch further may wish to moderate the strength of his stock while ensuring that the end product is still recognisably whisky. In which case, he will ask himself: 'To dilute stock of proof X in order to achieve proof, how much water must I add?'

YE'LL TAK THE MORAY ROAD

Although best known as a Shakespearean character, Macbeth was in fact a real Scottish king, who fatally wounded his predecessor King Duncan at the Battle of Burghead in 1040. The dying old king was carried to Elgin on the old road that now passes through the Glen Moray distillery, a road that has borne many a famous soul. Bonnie Prince Charlie marched along it with his army on their way to defeat at Culloden in 1745, while Dr Johnson and his faithful chum Boswell wandered down it some 30 years later on a tour of the area.

LUCKY LORD

When the secretary general of NATO, Lord Robertson of Port Ellen, visited Ardbeg Distillery on the Scottish island of Islay, in April 2000, the occasion was marked in a special way. To commemorate his visit, a cask of Ardbeg was filled in his presence and laid down in the warehouse for bottling in 2010. Particularly apt, as Lord Robertson's middle name is none other than Islay!

WHISKY IN FILM

Anna Christie, 1930
Greta Garbo made her speaking debut in Anna Christie. The public was kept in suspense for the first 20 minutes of the film and then Garbo uttered the immortal words:
'Gimme a whisky with ginger ale and don't be stingy, baby.'

True Grit, 1970
John Wayne's only Oscar Leading Actor win was for his portrayal of an eye-patched, whisky-guzzling deputy Marshall.

Live and Let Die, 1973
Roger Moore takes over as the new James Bond and the producers made a conscious effort to adjust the character made famous by Sean Connery. Moore's Bond drinks bourbon whiskey, not a vodka martini.

BEWARE BLONDIES

For those not familiar with Scottish New Year celebrations, Hogmanay traditions include something for the whisky lover. The Scottish lore of First Footing holds that the New Year will be a prosperous one, as long as on the stroke of midnight a tall dark stranger appears at your door with a lump of coal in his hand. A remote possibility you may think, but such is the tradition. But these days to ensure the first foot over the door is one of a suitable calibre, groups of friends and family get together and tour each others' houses. The bearer of the coal is traditionally met with a dram of whisky or a 'het pint', literally a 'hot pint' which consists of beer, nutmeg, eggs and whisky. Not a bad prize for a lump of coal.

And why the desire for a dark stranger to darken your door? Well apparently the fear of blond strangers comes from the fair haired Vikings who raped and pillaged their way across Scotland all those centuries ago.

Here's an example of London journalist and whisky fanatic Alfred Barnard's brilliant and meticulous reporting:

Established more than a century ago, Port Dundas has, by the energy and enterprise displayed by its founder, Robert Macfarlane, and latterly by his son Daniel, been so developed that it has become one of the largest Distilleries in the world; and although amalgamated with the Distillers' Company, Limited, Richard Macfarlane, son of the Daniel before mentioned, is now Managing Director for the Company at this Distillery. The works, covering nine acres of ground, are situated on a steep hill near to and overlooking the city of Glasgow and surrounding districts, and are close to the railway and canal. Having previously communicated by telephone with Mr. W. Bruce, the operative manager, we found that gentleman waiting to receive us. Under his guidance we commenced our inspection at the Barns or Granaries, situated at the north end of the Distillery on the higher slopes of the hill. They consist of buildings, four stories high, and same idea of their magnitude may be formed by the following facts. Number One at the time of Our visit contained 10,000 quarters of American corn, and Number Two, 14,000 quarters of barley and rye, and then they were not even full; at times they have stored as many as 45,000 quarters. The grain is imported by rail, canal, and carts, direct into the works, where it is emptied into hoppers, and taken by elevators and screws to any part of the buildings at will. We next entered the two malting floors, which are situated at the west end of the Granaries, and were amazed at their dimensions; they are quite the size of feeding parks, and a volunteer regiment could drill in them with ease.

The cisterns connected with these buildings each wet 2,400 bushels at one time. South of the Granaries, standing all in a line, are the seven Kilns, which are of great dimensions, one of them drying 2,000 quarters of grain at a time. Five of them are used for grain, the other two for malt, and all are heated by hot air. The dried malt and grain is then passed through screws to the malt and grain Store-rooms, five in number, each capable of holding 14,000 bushels of malt, and used alternately. The grain and malt passes from these rooms into the Mill, which building has the appearance of having been hewn out of a rock, nothing being seen but solid masonry and iron girders, 'i while it is covered by a large water tank communicating with all parts of the works where fire might originate, and capable of flooding the whole place in a few minutes. In the Mill there are eight pairs of large mill-stones, working night and day, driven by a powerful engine, upwards of 150 horse power.

The perils of drinking beer rather than whisky!

TREASURED ISLAND

There's many a murky past in the distillery tales of yore. Take, for example, the original Ardbeg distillery on the rocky south coast of the island of Islay, in western Scotland, and established by the McDougall family in 1815. It had previously been the site of illicit distillers and smugglers who were finding ways around the 1713 English malt tax. For years the excisemen knew of the illegal distillery's existence, knew where it was, and even knew by face the distillers themselves. But because the smuggling band was so large, they didn't have the manpower to tackle them.

So they simply waited one night until the men had set sail for the mainland with their latest cargo of whisky, raided the island, and destroyed the distillery. But so fine was the site and so perfect the waters for distilling, that when the McDougall family decided to set up Ardbeg, they picked the same spot and started business – legally!

THE TALLEST STILLS IN SCOTLAND

While traditional whisky stills are small and squat in their design, Glenmorangie Distillery has the tallest stills in Scotland, standing at an impressive 5.14 metres.

Glenmorangie's founder, William Matheson, was a 'canny' Scot and rather than purchase new stills, he saw an opportunity to buy second-hand gin stills. His decision in 1843 has continued to influence the Glenmorangie we know today. The eight stills in Glenmorangie's 'cathedral' of a still house are exact replicas of Matheson's original gin still.

INGREDIENTS FOR SUCCESS

Scotch Rickey

A dram of Scotch
A dash of lime juice
A dash of lemon juice
Ice
Soda

DRAM-ATIC WRITING

A TEN minutes' walk from our hotel, along Buchanan Street, the finest thoroughfare in Glasgow, and through busy Argyle Street, across the beautiful bridge which spans the Clyde, and we find ourselves at the Adelphi Distillery. Sixty-five years ago the site upon which it stands was a fine orchard, but in 1826 the trees were cut down to make room for the Distillery. The works cover upwards of two acres of ground, and are situated close to the banks of the Clyde. The course of this noble river, through the heart of the city, forms one of the most striking panoramas of its kind in the United Kingdom. From the centre of Jamaica Bridge, the scene presented to the ere is one never to be forgotten; a forest of masts extending as far as the ere can reach; the open centre of the silver stream; the wharves piled with wares from every nation, and alive with men from all parts of the world; the continuous flow of passengers passing to and from the various steamers; and the endless variety of sounds and sights complete a picture unequalled in any other city in the world. The bustle and activity of modern days is here seen to its fullest advantage.

Alfred Barnard, *The Whisky Distilleries of the United Kingdom*, 1887

SWANSONG

Eating sandwiches and sipping Jack Daniel's whiskey in the Korean countryside was one of the few real pleasures of being America's ambassador to that particular country in the 1950s. Senior American staff from the ambassador down through the senior military personnel had access to an almost limitless supply of whiskey and by all accounts they made use of it.

On one occasion the ambassador and half a dozen friends set off in search of wild swans to shoot. Reaching the sea wall of the Naktong delta, they peered over and saw more than two hundred magnificent swans swimming gently on the water. Eventually the birds took off in their distinctive V-shaped flying formation. With every wing-beat they climbed higher into the crisp blue sky. As they passed over the ambassador and his fellow guns there was a volley of shots, but the great birds carried on unmolested. The hunters were so drunk that they couldn't hit a barn swallow, let alone a swan.

Like most Americans in Korea at that time they were almost permanently under the influence – one officer later wrote that he had been drunk for months on end with the constant slow sipping filling up long days of boredom and as a result everything he tried to do – from shooting to chess – had turned into a pleasant if incompetent blur.

Jack Daniel's rations were much reduced for Vietnam and other subsequent conflicts.

THE HARD STUFF

What is the brewer's role in the whisky-making business?
Answer on page 153.

INDIGNITY

An old colonel who used to shoot pheasants while on leave from the Indian army in the remote north of the country, always carried at least two full bottles of whisky with him. His argument was that while out shooting there was a very real risk of breaking one bottle but you would have to be unusually unlucky to break both before you had time to drink them.

Asked why he didn't simply put his whisky in an unbreakable pewter or silver hip-flask he insisted that drinking whisky from metal was 'beneath the dignity of a soldier and gentleman'.

TOAST OF THE PAPERBACK SLEUTHS

Her name's Jack Daniels. Or, Lieutenant Jacqueline Daniels of the Chicago Police Department. She is the heroine of two novels by former improv comic and website designer, JA Konrath – and she gets into some nasty scrapes. In her first adventure, *Whiskey Sour* (2004), the hard-bitten, 40-something divorcee is pitted against The Gingerbread Man, a sadistic killer who has planned to murder four women in one week.

The sequel should help you to work out that Jack won through – but *Bloody Mary* (2005), finds her receiving a personal message in the form of two severed arms joined together by her own handcuffs. In the manner of the film *Seven*, the killer is caught with a fair stretch of the story left to tell, and Jack is left to make sure that he gets his just desserts.

Like a great deal of fiction written purely for enjoyment, Konrath's tales have found favour with genre fans over the heads of critics, and have been compared to the satirical novels of Carl Hiassen. So why not pick up a measure of Jack off the shelf?

INGREDIENTS FOR SUCCESS

Scotch Horse's Neck

A dram of Scotch
A dash of Angostura
Lemon juice
Ginger Ale

HAIR-RAISING

For the very hairy there is a point at which drinking can become decidedly messy and unpleasant, at least for spectators. This was a particularly aggravating problem for Victorians who spent years cultivating long, elaborate and sometimes very bushy moustaches and then drank to excess – whisky was a particular problem as its smell lingered for days if the drinker was unlucky enough to dribble.

So a particularly enterprising manufacturer came up with the idea of a moustache protector – a device that looked rather like a semi-circular curved piece of smooth metal with an oval hole in the middle. This moustache protector was carried by the moustache wearer wherever he (or conceivably she) went. As soon as a glass of whisky hove into view, he would take out his moustache protector and attach it to the edge of his tumbler and drink through the small hole; the metal flange round the hole in the protector ensuring the pristine survival of the facial hair.

WIT AND WHISKY

Q: What is the fastest way to get stoned?
A: Whisky on the rocks

THE HARD STUFF

How is the alcoholic strength of Scotch whisky measured?
Answer on page 153.

WHISKY ON THE BRAIN

Those splendid pith helmets that we associate with the knobbly knees, the huge pairs of short trousers and the bad-tempered habits of old colonels in India and Africa were absolutely vital to the maintenance of the Empire.

Much thought and effort was expended on their manufacture because, however determined the British were to bring the solid values of the Home Counties to those less well-favoured parts of the world, it could only be done if the poor blighters doing the work were protected adequately from the sun. Which is why one bright spark thought it would be rather good if pith helmets could carry their own water supply.

The all-purpose water helmet, advertised in a number of late nineteenth-century magazines was built high and wide with a gentle slope down to a wide brim. At the bottom of the slope all the way round and at the edge of the brim was a deep gutter. On those rare occasions when it rained in the tropics the water would collect in the gutter and then run into a specially-made miniature tank at the back of the hat and below the gutter. The tank protected the neck from the sun and could store almost a pint of water.

When the wearer felt a little thirsty he took the hat off, turned it around and undid a small brass tap fitted to the tank at the back. This released the collected water which, we are reliably informed, could be used 'either to refresh the palate or to cool the brow.'

But a large drawback quickly became apparent – all those who used the hat immediately filled it up with whatever alcohol was available and since the hat was largely the prerequisite of military officers whose favourite drink was whisky, the hats were used as a sort of moveable bar. It was reported that the efficiency of Her Majesty's officers rapidly declined.

SPECIAL DIET

Perhaps the most extraordinary alternative to steam power was the 1830s patent for an ingenious system by which a carriage was to be drawn along the line 'by the muscular power of the two guards who constantly accompany it'.

The carriage was described as very light and elegant in appearance, and capable of carrying seven or eight passengers at the rate of 18 miles an hour.

'We have no doubt,' says the patent document, 'that these men will need no uncommon diet – we recommend a diet of meat, fish and whisky.'

BEST SELLING

Quick stats about whisky sales

- One in every five bottles of single malt sold in the world is Glennfiddich.

- Greeks drink more Scotch whisky per person than any other country in the world.

- Johnnie Walker Red Label is the largest-selling brand of Scotch whisky in the world.

SMALL BEER, BIG WHISKY

Glen Moray Distillery is situated on the banks of the River Lossie, which supplies it with water, in the city of Elgin, the historical capital of Speyside in north-east Scotland, a region synonymous with malt whisky. Glen Moray single malt whisky has been distilled here since 1897 by a small, dedicated team of craftsmen. But it wasn't always so. Built in 1815, Glen Moray was originally a brewery before its conversion. There's no accounting for taste.

The distillery was acquired by Macdonald & Muir in 1923 and rebuilt in 1958 and converted from two to four stills. Although over the years the distilling technology has changed, the ingredients and processes remain the same to ensure a best-selling, quality whisky. The ex-bourbon barrels used to mature Glen Moray give it a rich, spicy flavour with a smooth, well-rounded taste.

Never trust a vicar who drinks Champagne. Whisky on the other hand makes even the worst feel godly.

WHISKY FOR WILLIE

Groundskeeper Willie is one of the many colourful inhabitants of Springfield, along with the Simpsons. Voiced by Dan Castellaneta he embodies just about every Scottish stereotype, with red hair, a thick accent and a partiality to a drink. Having worked at the elementary school for over 20 years, Willie has developed a distinct dislike of children, possibly down to Bart's pranks. In one memorable episode Bart attached helium balloons to Willie's kilt, revealing his true Scottish habit of not wearing anything underneath.

Willie is also more than partial to some Scotch food, being especially fond of a bit of haggis and whisky – so much so that he keeps a hip-flask on him at all times. A nip of whisky has come in handy considering some of the scrapes Willie has become involved in – from saving Bart from a predatory wolf by wrestling it into submission to taking part in a successful expedition to capture the Loch Ness Monster. All in a day's work when you live near Homer Simpson.

THE SIXTEEN MEN OF TAIN

The Glenmorangie Distillery remains one of the most traditional in the Highlands of Scotland, employing just 16 craftsmen – 'The Sixteen Men of Tain'. Their experience, craft and traditional values have been passed down the generations since 1843. Glenmorangie continues to be handcrafted at the Distillery in Tain, in the Highlands of Scotland.

THE CONSUMPTION OF WHISKY...

...may leave you wondering what the hell happened to your bra and panties.

...may make you think you are whispering when you are not.

...may cause you to tell your friends over and over again that you love them.

...may cause you to think you can sing.

...may lead you to believe that ex-lovers are really dying for you to telephone them at four in the morning.

...may make you think you can logically converse with members of the opposite sex without spitting.

...may create the illusion that you are tougher, smarter, faster and better-looking than most people.

...may lead you to think people are laughing with you.

...may cause pregnancy.

...may be a major factor in getting your ass kicked.

...may Mack you tink you kan type reel gode.

TWO OLD CAT TALES

Distillery bosses from the Grouse Glenturret plant at Crieff in Perthshire, central Scotland, believe the nip of whisky given in milk each night to their fiery feline, Towser, could have helped him achieve his record-breaking tally of 30,000 mice caught in his 24-year lifetime. A bronze statue was erected in his honour at the plant and a cat psychologist was consulted in the search for the successor to the incredible mousing moggie after his death in 2005.

Meanwhile, in Essex, Whiskey is the name of Britain's oldest cat. Rescued as a kitten from a litter bin in 1971, Whiskey was still going strong in 2005 having attained the grand old age of 231... in cat years!

DURING THE COMPILATION OF THIS BOOK,
THE COMPANION TEAM...

Travelled the length and breadth of Britain, falling in peaty burns, stumbling down dangerous crags and camping on damp hillsides to sample the rarest and most obscure malts in the open air where they would almost certainly have originally have been drunk

Drank fine whiskies with pickled anchovies, Stilton cheese, habanero chillies, kimchee (Korean pickled cabbage) and bangalore phal chicken to see if they brought out any interesting flavours in the whisky (they didn't)

Flew at high altitude to see if the whisky would disappear by evaporation, but drank it before the experiment could get under way

Soaked our feet in single malt to see if it would prevent blisters during walks across the Highlands (it didn't)

Tried the old gunpowder proof test by setting fire to a fine whisky – it burned beautifully, but oh Lord, what a waste

Tried blending our own whisky. Never again

Visited a voice coach to see if she thought we could sing better after a few drams

Tried making whisky ice-cream – absolutely delicious

Experimented with three bald heads to discover if whisky makes hair grow, and turned three still-bald men drunk by osmosis

Tried to find out if whisky ever goes off once opened, but couldn't leave it alone long enough

Please note that although every effort has been made to ensure accuracy in this book, the above facts may be the result of tired and emotional minds.

I like my whisky old and my women young.

Errol Flynn

The answers. As if you needed them.

P 16.   Spirit of proof was the way alcoholic strength was measured until 1980. This began in the late seventeenth century when whisky and gunpowder were mixed and lit. If the mix exploded, the whisky was held to have been proofed. If the spirit was too weak there was no explosion and the whisky had not been proofed. By the 1740s, distillers had begun to use Clarks hydrometer to measure spirit strength. Then came the Sikes system, a highly accurate hydrometer, which was adopted in 1816 and retained till 1980.

P 21.   Balvenie

P 28.   95%

P 37.   Blending

P 48.   Scotch whisky sold in the UK must be bottled at 40% ABV; Scotch whisky sold overseas must be bottled at 43% ABV.

P 55.   Malt whisky is made by the pot still process; grain whisky by the patent still (or Coffey still) process. Malt whisky is made only from malted barley; grain whisky is made using a small proportion of malted barley and maize or wheat.

P 62.   The Customs and Excise Act of 1952 defined spirits of proof strength as follows: 'Spirits shall be deemed to be at proof if the volume of the ethyl alcohol contained therein made up to the volume of the spirits with distilled water has a weight equal to that of twelve-thirteenths of a volume of distilled water equal to the volume of the spirits, the volume of each liquid being computed as at fifty-one degrees Fahrenheit.' In other words, proof spirit meant that the spirit at a temperature of 51°F, weighed exactly 12/13 of a volume of distilled water equal to the volume of the spirit. It was, in fact, a mixture of spirit and water of a strength of 57.1% of spirit by volume and 42.9% of water.

P 70.   Whisky has to be allowed to mature for at least three years. After blending, Scotch is usually returned to a cask for a few months so the mixture can meld together before being bottled.

P 75.   Yes – at Gwalia distillery, in the Brecon Beacons, Wales.

P 83.   Malt whiskies have a far stronger flavour than grain whiskies because their taste is dependent on local conditions of peat and water. Grain whisky has little taste variation linked to geographical factors. But no one really knows exactly why whisky tastes as it does. Alcohol, oils from the barley, water and traces from peat and the barrels in which it matures all combine. Water is key, too, because the rich peaty water of Islay for example, is far stronger in taste than the many mainland sources of water.

P 91. He was an exciseman. In other words he was employed to catch illegal whisky distillers!

P 103. Glendalough – it's a place in Ireland, not a whisky.

P 113. The product of a single distillery.

P 115. Roughly 1860 when Andrew Usher made the first blend in Edinburgh.

P 129. No – whisky has to be at least three years old before it can be sold.

P 135. 15 years

P 145. The brewer is the person in charge of the fermentation process which produces an alcoholic liquid known as wash, around 7-10% alcohol by volume.

P 147. In common with other EU countries, on 1 January 1980, Britain adopted the system of measurement recommended by the International Organisation of Legal Metrology, a body with most major nations among its members. The OIML system measures alcoholic strength as a percentage of alcohol by volume at a temperature of 20°C. It replaced the Sikes system of measuring the proof strength of spirits, which had been used in Britain for over 160 years.

TASTING NOTES

Happiness is having a rare steak, a bottle of whisky, and a dog to eat the rare steak.

Johnny Carson

ACKNOWLEDGEMENTS

We gratefully acknowledge permission to reprint extracts of copyright material in this book from the following authors, publishers and executors:

The Smuggler's Song by Rudyard Kipling reproduced by permission of AP Watt Ltd on behalf on the National Trust for Places of Historic Interest or Natural Beauty.

The Whisky Distilleries of the United Kingdom by Alfred Barnard, 1887.

The Birdwatcher's Companion Twitchers, birders and ornithologists are all catered for in this unique book. ISBN 1-86105-833-0

The Cook's Companion Foie gras or fry-ups, this tasty compilation is an essential ingredient in any kitchen. ISBN 1-86105-772-5

The Countryside Companion From milking stools to crofters tools, this book opens the lid on the rural scene. ISBN 1-86105-918-3

The Fishing Companion This fascinating catch of fishy facts offers a whole new angle on angling. ISBN 1-86105-919-1

The Gardener's Companion For anyone who has ever gone in search of flowers, beauty and inspiration. ISBN 1-86105-771-7

The Golfer's Companion From plus fours to six irons, here's where to find the heaven and hell of golf. ISBN 1-86105-834-9

The History of Britain Companion All the oddities, quirks, origins and stories that make our country what it is today. ISBN 1-86105-914-0

The Ideas Companion The stories behind the trademarks, inventions, and brands that we come across every day. ISBN 1-86105-835-7

The Legal Companion From lawmakers to lawbreakers, find out all the quirks and stories behind the legal world. ISBN 1-86105-838-1

The Literary Companion Literary fact and fiction from Rebecca East to Vita Sackville-West. ISBN 1-86105-798-9

The London Companion Explore the history and mystery of the most exciting capital city in the world. ISBN 1-86105-799-7

The Moviegoer's Companion Movies, actors, cinemas and salty popcorn in all their glamorous glory. ISBN 1-86105-797-0

The Politics Companion Great leaders and greater liars of international politics gather round the hustings. ISBN 1-86105-796-2

The Sailing Companion Starboards, stinkpots, raggie and sterns – here's where to find out more. ISBN 1-86105-839-X

The Shakespeare Companion A long, hard look at the man behind the moustache and his plethora of works. ISBN 1-86105-913-2

The Traveller's Companion For anyone who's ever stared at a plane and spent the day dreaming of faraway lands. ISBN 1-86105-773-3

The Walker's Companion Ever laced a sturdy boot and stepped out in search of stimulation? This book is for you. ISBN 1-86105-825-X

The Wildlife Companion Animal amazements and botanical beauties abound in this book of natural need-to-knows. ISBN 1-86105-770-9